ACTIVE FIRST AID

Second Edition

© 2003-2007 Active Publications Pty Limited
ISBN 1-920929-00-2

By Peter Mᶜkie

Text revised to meet the latest guidelines from the Resuscitation Council UK and the European Resuscitation Council.

Disclaimer

The information contained in this manual relates to the current accepted first aid practices in the Europe and United Kingdom at the time of publication. It does not provide information about first aid practices in any country other than the United Kingdom.

This manual is an information resource only and is not a substitute for undertaking a first aid course.

While every effort has been made to ensure that the information is accurate at the time of publication, the authors are not responsible for any loss, liability, damage or injury that may be suffered or incurred by any person in connection with the information contained in this book, or by anyone who receives first aid treatment from a reader or user of this book.

Published by
Active Publications Limited
29 Harley Street
London W1G 9QR

Email: info@activepublications.co.uk
Web: http://www.activepublications.co.uk

Printed in the United Kingdom

Distributed by the First Aid Cafe

Printed: June 2007

CONTENTS

INTRODUCTION

What makes a good First Aid Text Book? Regardless of how many words, how good the pictures, how technical the information, a good First Aid Text Book must be easy to read, logically set out and must welcome the reader or student the first and every time they pick it up, not frighten them away with complexity.

Active First Aid by Peter MCkie fulfils all these criteria. Now in its 2nd Edition, the text is clear, concise and simple to read, with excellent pictures and illustrations and colour-coded sections enhance user-friendliness.

The key to successful first aid is having a simple, consistent approach to a variety of common and predictable situations, and the knowledge and "game-plan" to apply to the unusual and unpredictable ones.

While this manual is a stand-alone resource, it is not the whole story: I would encourage every person to attend a first aid training course, cement the knowledge contained in this book and perfect the practical first aid techniques described within. The greatest gift you can give anyone is their life.

Kind personal regards,

DR. ADRIAN COHEN

Dr. Adrian Cohen is a medical educator, television presenter and pre-hospital care expert. His company, Immediate Assistants, is a Recognised Training Organisation and is the medical services provider for the hit CBS television "Survivor" series, major sporting events as well as Film/TV productions and large sporting venues.

HOW TO USE THIS MANUAL

This quick guide has been designed to help in most emergency situations by providing simple to follow information and treatment guides.

The guide introduces first aid, covers the essentials of first aid and the most common trauma and medical emergencies.

It is ideal for first aid kits, at work, or at home.

While this manual is a valuable resource, we encourage every person to attend a first aid course at their earliest convenience.

We also advise that everyone have a first aid kit for home and in the car.

Colour bars help you find relevant sections.

Caution icon advises you of how to avoid further risks to the casualty.

Introduction gives a brief explanation of the topic.

Magnifying glass icon for quick reference to signs & symptoms.

First aid cross icon quickly directs you to the 'how to treat' information.

Colour graphics provide additional visual information.

30 | First Aid Quick Guide

SEIZURES

Epilepsy is a disruption of brain function that interrupts the normal electrical activity of the brain.

SIGNS AND SYMPTOMS
- sudden loss of consciousness
- staring blankly ahead
- odd noises or movement such as chewing or smacking lips
- localised twitching or jerking
- stiffening and muscle jerking
- breathing ceases (resumes once seizure has finished)
- pale, blue/grey skin colour
- clenched jaw, with saliva around mouth, may be blood tinged
- incontinence
- after seizure casualty may feel tired and fall asleep

CARE AND TREATMENT
- protect from harm
- place something soft under head
- loosen any tight clothing
- roll into recovery position when jerking stops
- reassure until fully recovered
- call '000' for an ambulance if required
- regularly monitor casualty

⚠ **DO NOT** put anything in the casualty's mouth, including fingers
⚠ **DO NOT** restrain casualty

Most epileptics *do not usually* require ambulance care and may become upset when one is called. However you must satisfy yourself that the person is recovering normally, with no apparent complications.

Febrile convulsions

Febrile convulsions occur when a child has a high temperature. The growing brains of small children are more sensitive to fever than are more mature brains and when the normal brain activity is upset a convulsion or 'fit' can occur.

SIGNS AND SYMPTOMS
- previous history of infection
- child is quiet and appears sick
- flushed, hot skin
- eyes 'roll back'
- may become stiff or floppy
- child becomes prostrate and begins convulsing
- salivary drool
- may become 'blue'
- after one to three minutes, child begins breathing normally
- recovers, commences crying

1 INTRODUCTION TO FIRST AID

- ✍ Principles of first aid
- ✍ First aid at work
- ✍ The human body
- ✍ First aid hygiene
- ✍ Examining a casualty
- ✍ Road traffic accidents
- ✍ Multiple casualties
- ✍ The chain of survival
- ✍ First aid kits

Emergencies can happen at any time and in any place, and a treatment delay of just a few minutes can mean death when the heart has stopped. When emergencies happen you need to know what to do, and the correct procedures to follow. This section introduces you to the basic concepts involved in first aid and the essential steps required to carry out adequate first aid.

By the end of this section you should be able to:

- ✚ Assess the casualty in an emergency situation.
- ✚ Initiate a call for help to emergency services.
- ✚ Understand your responsibilities in the workplace.
- ✚ Correctly document your first aid treatment.
- ✚ Identify the basic systems in the human body.
- ✚ Recognise the importance of hygiene in first aid.
- ✚ Demonstrate the steps involved in the examination of a casualty.
- ✚ Manage a multiple casualty situation.
- ✚ Identify the *'mechanism of injury'* in road traffic accidents.
- ✚ Identify the four links in the 'Chain of Survival'.
- ✚ Understand the importance of first aid kits.
- ✚ Recognise the basic items in a first aid kit.

PRINCIPLES OF FIRST AID

First aid is the initial assistance or care of a suddenly sick or injured person. It is the vital initial care we all feel an impulse to give as soon as possible after an accident or illness.

First aid is an important part of everyday life, both at home, work or at play. Everyone should learn first aid and be willing to administer basic care until emergency assistance arrives. Not every incident requiring first aid is a life-and-death situation. First aid knowledge is commonly used to manage minor injuries at home or work.

What is first aid?

First aid is the immediate care of an injured or suddenly sick person. It is the care a person applies as soon as possible after an accident or sudden illness.

This prompt care and attention prior to the arrival of the ambulance can sometimes mean the difference between life and death, or between a full or partial recovery.

The main aims of first aid are to:

1. Preserve life - This includes the life of the casualty, bystander and rescuer.
2. Protect the casualty from further harm - Ensure the scene is safe.
3. Provide pain relief - This could include the use of ice packs or simply applying a sling.
4. Prevent the injury or illness from becoming worse - Ensure that the treatment you provide does not make the condition worse.
5. Provide reassurance

It is important to understand that first aid has its limitations and does not take the place of professional medical treatment.

Immediate action

Taking immediate action is the essential principle in first aid. Bystanders or relatives may not recognise the basic symptoms of an injury or illness and may wait hours before calling for help. Often people are worried about "doing the wrong thing", so don't attempt any first aid at all. If a person is sick or injured, then they need help, and they need it immediately.

A casualty who is not breathing effectively, or is bleeding heavily, requires immediate aid. Prompt effective first aid gives the casualty a much better chance of a good recovery.

It is important that prompt action does not lead to panic, and the first aider should form a plan of action. Careful and deliberate action undertaken without too much delay is most beneficial to the casualty. Try to remain calm and think your actions through. A calm and controlled first aider will give everyone confidence that the event is being handled efficiently and effectively.

Each emergency is different, so it is impossible to provide you with a precise list of things you need to do for every emergency. However, if you follow the 'principles of first aid' as outlined, you should deliver appropriate care, even if you are not sure of what the underlying problem is.

Getting help

In the UK dial **'999'** for emergency assistance such as *ambulance, fire, police, coastguard* or *rescue services*.

You can dial **'999'** from any phone, fixed or mobile.

Alternative ways to call for help

You can also use **112** anywhere in the European Community to contact emergency services

Another feature of the 112 system is that it can be dialled from anywhere in the world with GSM coverage and is then automatically translated to that country's emergency number.

In a workplace there may be an internal number to call in an emergency which should be clearly displayed on or around the telephone.

Motorways have emergency phones that can be found every mile, and blue and white marker posts are placed in between them, with an arrow to point you in the direction of the nearest phone. These are linked to motorway police control centres, allowing them to pinpoint your position and get help to you quickly.

There are many other methods of calling for help that can be considered when a telephone is not available. These include:

○ satellite phones ○ HF/VHF radio
○ two way radio ○ e-mail
○ flags ○ flares
○ Personal Locator Beacons (EPIRBS)

If you are attending to a casualty, have a bystander telephone for help. If you are on your own you may have to leave the casualty for a short time to make a call.

The specific circumstance surrounding the incident will dictate whether you call for help, or whether you send a bystander.

You should instruct the bystander to give some basic information to the operator, and get them to repeat it back to you to ensure that the correct information is understood. The caller should return and inform the first aider that help has been called.

There are 3 important things to remember when calling for help:

1. State which emergency service you require: Ambulance, Fire, or Police.

2. Stay on the line until connected with the emergency service operator as they will need to talk to you before sending assistance.

3. Give as much information as possible about the location of the emergency. The information required will depend on whether you are in an urban or rural area, and include:

❏ exact address or location
   ➲ street/road name and number
   ➲ suburb, city/town
   ➲ nearest cross road or street
   ➲ landmarks
   ➲ distance from landmark, intersection or roadside box/number
❏ phone number from where the call is being made
❏ what happened – eg car accident

□ number and condition of the casualties, including level of consciousness, breathing and circulation.

□ any hazards present

The dispatcher may give you information of how to treat the casualty until assistance arrives.

As an example, you might say that you require an ambulance at 27 Smith Street in Banbury, Oxfordshire and that you have a 45 year old male who has fallen approximately 3 metres and struck his head. He was unconscious for a short time but is conscious now and that he has a history of asthma.

Medical identification tags

As a form of assistance and notification, people with medical conditions may wear or carry a form of medical identification, usually a bracelet, necklace or a card in their wallet.

These medical-alert devices are imprinted with the person's identity, the relevant medical condition, allergies, drugs required and specialised medical contact information.

Medical conditions that may be shown vary from specific heart diseases, to diabetes, epilepsy, asthma, and serious allergies.

Reassurance

The psychological value of reassurance is as important in first aid as the treatment that you give. Comfort and reassure the casualty, as in some cases all the casualty needs is emotional support and reassurance.

A calm approach by the first aider and keeping the casualty informed of what is happening will also assist in the reassurance process.

Remember that many people who have assisted you in delivering care to an injured or ill casualty may need reassurance themselves. Relatives of the casualty may be concerned that they let the casualty down or that they made a mistake in not getting help earlier; workmates may feel that they contributed little to helping the casualty; onlookers may feel guilty that they provided only a little practical assistance.

Take some time out at the end of the incident to tell people how important their contribution was. Let them know that effectively caring for a casualty is a team effort and that every little job counts. This is especially true if the outcome of the emergency was unsuccessfull.

Your response to an emergency

An emergency of any size can cause unusual stress in people who have been directly and indirectly affected by it. Every person will react differently and a range of responses to an emergency is normal, and to be expected. Emotional responses to disasters can appear immediately or sometimes months later. Understanding what you're feeling and taking positive steps can help you cope with this disaster.

Some common responses to emergencies and disasters are:

- ❒ Crying for "no apparent reason"
- ❒ Difficulty making decisions
- ❒ Difficulty sleeping
- ❒ Disbelief, shock, irritability, anger, disorientation, apathy, emotional numbing, sadness and depression
- ❒ Excessive drinking or drug use
- ❒ Extreme hunger or lack of appetite
- ❒ Fear and anxiety about the future
- ❒ Feeling powerless
- ❒ Flashbacks
- ❒ Headaches and stomach problems

If you have strong feelings that won't go away or if you are troubled for longer than four to six weeks, you may want to seek professional help.

The clean up

After an incident it is important to put some time aside for yourself. Very often first aiders become concerned that they did not do a good enough job and that they were not effective in their role.

When you think about how you handled the incident, the first thing you should keep in mind is that by stepping forward and doing first aid you have done more for the casualty than anyone else could ever do.

As the great humanitarian Albert Schweitzer said, *"The purpose of life is to serve and show compassion and the will to help others."*

In dealing with the aftermath of the incident, go and get a cup of tea and talk to a family member, friend or colleague.

When you go over how you handled the incident, be realistic about your expectations. Time must also be allocated to the clean up of the scene and equipment, and to restock your first aid kit. You should:

- ❒ Take a break
- ❒ Talk about the incident with peers
- ❒ Try to relax as much as possible
- ❒ Clean up the scene
- ❒ Clean up any equipment used
- ❒ Restock your first aid kit:
    - ⊃ replace all items used
    - ⊃ look for any soiled unopened items that will need to be replaced
- ❒ Complete any documentation
- ❒ Securely file documentation

FIRST AID AT WORK

The information in this chapter is a guide only. It is provided to help first aiders understand the potential legal consequences of becoming involved in an incident. You should seek your own independent legal advice if you have any specific questions about legal issues associated with first aid procedures or become involved in legal action.

Every employer and self-employed person, has a duty to make provision for first aid in their workplace, as described in The Health and Safety (First-Aid) Regulations 1981 and Approved Code of Practice and Guidance, L74 1997.

The Health and Safety (First Aid) Regulations 1981 set out the essential aspects of first aid that employers have to address. The Regulations describe the duties of employers to make first-aid provision for their employees.

Although the first aid regulations are only applicable to employees, the Health & Safety Executive (HSE) recommends that other people such as customers or contract workers are taken into account, when assessing first aid provision.

First-aid at work is about the preservation of life, minimising the consequences of injury or illness and the treatment of minor injuries. It is not about providing medical facilities, services or treatment, or the administration of medicines. The objective is to ensure employers have made the appropriate arrangements for workers who are injured or taken ill at work to receive immediate attention and to ensure that an ambulance is called in serious cases.

There is a legal requirement to report and document accidents and ill health at work. Serious accidents are reportable under RIDDOR which is the Reporting of Injuries, Diseases and Dangerous Occurrences Regulations. You need to report:

❑ Deaths
❑ Major injuries
❑ Accidents resulting in over 3 day injury
❑ Diseases
❑ Dangerous occurrences
❑ Gas incidents

You must notify the Incident Contact Centre without delay, either telephone (0845 3009923) or via the RIDDOR website (www.riddor.gov.uk).

The employer should ensure that an employee who is injured or taken ill at work receives immediate attention, as in the event of sudden illness or injuries, failure to provide first aid could result in that person's death.

There are five main legal considerations relating to first aid:

❑ Tablets and medications
❑ Duty of Care
❑ Negligence
❑ Consent
❑ Recording

Tablets and medications

The HSE guidance material states that *first aid at work* does not include giving tablets or medications to treat illness and such items should not be kept in the first aid box. However, strictly speaking, there is no legal bar to employers making such items available to employees, if the *assessment of first aid needs* indicates they should be provided.

HSE has no objection to paracetamol or aspirin being made available in the workplace. First aiders issuing these tablets should have a reasonable understanding of what is involved.

Some workers carry their own medications such as inhalers for asthma or 'EpiPens' which contain injectable adrenaline for the treatment of severe allergic (anaphylactic) reactions, for example to peanuts. These medications are prescribed by a doctor. If an individual needs to take their own prescribed medication, the first aider's role is limited to helping them do so and contacting the emergency services as appropriate.

Medicines legislation restricts the administration of injectable medicines. Unless self administered, they may only be administered by or in accordance with the instructions of a doctor (eg by a nurse).

However, in the case of adrenaline there is an exemption to this restriction which means in an emergency, a suitably trained lay person is permitted to administer it by injection for the purpose of saving life.

The use of an EpiPen to treat anaphylactic shock falls into this category. Therefore, first aiders may administer an EpiPen if they are dealing with a life threatening emergency in a casualty who has been prescribed and is in possession of an EpiPen and where the first aider is trained to use it.

Reference: *http://www.hse.gov.uk/firstaid/faqs.htm*

Duty of care

"Duty of care" describes the legal duty owed by one person to another to act in a certain way. As a first aider, you have a duty of care towards your casualties to exercise reasonable care and skill in providing first aid treatment. The duty arises because you have knowledge and skills relevant to a medical emergency situation.

If you choose to provide first aid assistance, you have a duty to use your knowledge and skills in a responsible way.

The common law does not impose an automatic duty on first aiders to go to the aid of every casualty they come across. However, first aiders do have a duty to provide first aid assistance if they have voluntarily taken on that role. For example, a nominated first aid officer in a workplace owes a duty of care to assist another person in that workplace.

Legislation can also impose a duty of care. Once you start first aid treatment of a casualty you do take on a duty of care to provide first aid with reasonable skill and care and ensure your actions do not increase the risk to the casualty. You should continue to provide first aid once this treatment has begun, until:

- ❏ The scene becomes unsafe
- ❏ Another trained first aider arrives and takes over
- ❏ Qualified help arrives and takes over
- ❏ The casualty shows signs of recovery
- ❏ You become physically unable to continue

Negligence

In the unlikely event that a first aider is sued in connection with providing first aid assistance, the courts would look at the circumstances surrounding the event to see if the first aider acted negligently in the way the first aid was provided. The following factors must all be present for a first aider to be found negligent:

1. A duty of care existed between the first aider and the casualty; and
2. The first aider did not exercise reasonable care and skill in providing the first aid; and
3. The casualty sustained damage; and

4. The casualty's damage was caused by the first aider.

A first aider is not considered a 'professional' in most cases. A court would look at the first aider's training and at what a prudent and reasonable person would have done with the same level of training in the same circumstances.

Because encouraging people to assist others is in the public interest, it is likely that the courts would only see first aiders as liable if it can be shown that their behaviour was grossly negligent and would take account of all the circumstances of the event.

The court may examine issues to establish whether the first aider exercised reasonable care, such as:

- ❐ What was the first aider's level of knowledge?
- ❐ Did the first aider perform within their skill levels.
- ❐ What information was available for the first aider, including:
    - ⊃ was adequate questioning used?
    - ⊃ was a thorough examination of the casualty undertaken?
    - ⊃ were all the facts available taken into account?
- ❐ Were accepted first aid procedures complied with?
- ❐ What were the circumstances in which the first aider provided assistance?

Example:

A first aider gives CPR to a casualty in cardiac arrest. During this CPR a rib is broken. The resuscitation is successful and after the event the casualty decides to sue for the rib injury.

The court would look at the facts and may decide that:

- ❐ It is reasonable to expect that a first aider might break a casualty's rib while delivering CPR to save the casualty's life; and
- ❐ The first aider acted with reasonable care and skill; and
- ❐ The first aider was not negligent in providing CPR in this way; and
- ❐ The outcome for the casualty of not performing CPR could have been far worse than suffering a broken rib.

Consent

Before you start treating a casualty you should ask for and receive the casualty's consent to your treatment. If the casualty is unconscious, or is unable to give consent due to their injuries, you can assume consent and start treatment. If the casualty is under 18 years old, then you should seek consent from a parent or guardian. If a parent or guardian is not present, you can start treatment.

You should not start treatment if an adult, who seems of sound mind and able to make a decision, refuses your offer of treatment.

You only have the casualty's consent to treat them for a condition that affects their immediate health. You should not provide help for any ailment that goes beyond your knowledge of first aid.

Recording

First aiders should always make notes or fill out a casualty report on any event attended, no matter how minor. Proper records will help you to recall the incident if you are ever asked about it at a later stage.

Reporting accidents and ill health at work is a legal requirement. The enforcing authorities use the information to see the big picture of where injuries, ill health and accidental losses are occurring, and to advise on preventive action.

It is good practice to provide your first aiders/appointed persons with a book in which to record incidents that required their attendance. It is usually the first aider or appointed person who looks after the book, but employers have overall responsibility.

Records may be used in a court, so ensure that your reports or notes are legible, accurate, factual, contain all relevant information, and are based on observations rather than opinions.

When preparing a report some general guidelines should be followed:

- ❏ Use ink only.
- ❏ Any corrections should be crossed out with a single line and initialled. Do not use correction fluid to correct any mistakes.
- ❏ Sign and date the record.
- ❏ The information should be kept confidential, and should only be accessed by authorised people.
- ❏ In a workplace incident, a copy should go to authorised employer representatives for auditing and OH&S monitoring purposes.

Documenting your treatment

The accurate recording of injury/illness is also of great assistance to any medical personnel who take over your casualty's treatment, such as ambulance officers.

The format that is used to report injury and illness varies from workplace to workplace.

The information which should be contained in an injury/illness report is:

- ❏ The date and time of incident
- ❏ Brief personal details (name, address, date of birth)
- ❏ History of the illness/injury
- ❏ Observations (signs, symptoms and vital signs)
- ❏ The first aider's assessment of the injury/illness
- ❏ Date
- ❏ Signature of first aider
- ❏ The date of report
- ❏ Print name and title of first aider

Copies of reports should be given to:

- ❏ The person taking over care
- ❏ The casualty

The first aider keeps a copy as a record which is to be kept secure.

 The confidentiality of all records must be maintained

A copy of the report should be sent with the casualty to the hospital or medical facility.

A sample injury/illness report form on the following page shows the essential amount of information required.

Useful Resources

Reporting of Injuries, Diseases and Dangerous Occurrences Regulations

http://www.riddor.gov.uk
☎ 0845 3009923

Injury/Illness Form

Date	Time	Location
5/2/2006	12:59pm	27 Smith Street, Banbury, Oxfordshire

Surname	Given Name		Date of Birth	Gender
Mckie	Peter		15/5/1958	Male

Address		City	County	Postcode
45 Bent Street		Banbury	Oxfordshire	OX

History of Injury/Illness

Male casualty fell off ladder on to concrete floor. Fell 3m hitting head first. Workmate stated that the casualty had brief period of unresponsiveness (?1 minute) prior to arrival.

Allergies	Medication
Penicillin	Ventolin

Observations	Time 1:15pm	Time 1:21pm	Time 1:27pm	Assessment
Level of Consciousness				
Fully Conscious	✔	✔	✔	**A**brasion
Drowsy				**B**urn
Unconscious				**C**ontusion
Pulse				**D**eformity
Rate	88	90	80	**F**racture
Description	strong	strong	strong	**H**aemorrhage
Breathing				**L**aceration
Rate	28	26	20	**P**ain
Description	regular	regular	regular	**R**igidity
Skin				**S**welling
Colour	Pale	Pink	Pink	**T**enderness

Assessment diagram annotations: SHP, CP

Other Observations

Assessment

Casualty complaining of pain to forehead and right arm. Swelling and bleeding to forehead. Contusion and pain to (R) forearm. Reduced movement to (R) forearm. Fully conscious on arrival with full recollection of accident.

Treatment

Reassurance. Laid flat with head and neck support. Dressing over wound to forehead. Immobilised (R) arm with arm sling. Observations.

Follow Up/Referral	Comments
✔ Ambulance	History of mild asthma
☐ Medical Centre	
☐ Own Doctor	
☐ Other	

White copy for administration
Pink copy for Doctor/Ambulance
Blue copy for casualty

First Aider: (Print) John Fahey .... Position:...........
Signature: John Fahey Date: 5/2/06 Time: 1:45pm

THE HUMAN BODY

The human body is composed of a number of **'systems'**, each with a specific role in the function of the body as a whole.

It is useful for a first aider to have a basic awareness of the major systems and their functions. Knowledge of human anatomy will assist you in a first aid diagnosis, and will also provide a firm basis for the care and treatment of a casualty.

Essentially, there are ten anatomical systems, with some more important than others. This section will address those systems that are of significance in first aid delivery.

The nervous system

The nervous system is considered in two main parts, the **Central Nervous System** and the **Peripheral Nervous System**.

The Central Nervous System comprises the brain and spinal cord. The brain controls all functions of the body, and is the most complex of all body systems. The brain regulates all body functions, including the respiratory and cardiovascular systems. The spinal cord delivers the signals to all parts of the body.

The motor and sensory nerves, which involve movement, are known as the Peripheral Nervous System, and these are directed by the brain. Some peripheral nerves function without conscious thought, and these are known as autonomic nerves. Breathing is a function that is attributable to these nerves.

The cardiovascular system

This system involves the **heart, blood vessels and blood**. The heart is the pump that drives the blood around the body. The body's main vessels are *arteries*, which take the blood from the heart, and *veins*, which return the blood to the heart.

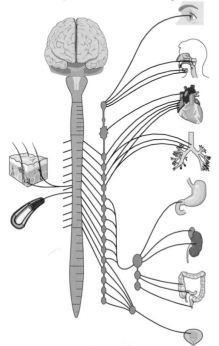

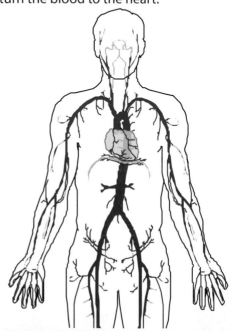

There are smaller blood vessels such as *arterioles*, *venules* and *capillaries*, most of which are located at the body's extremities and usually close to the skin.

Blood is the medium that transports oxygen, from the respiratory system to the body's cells. Blood also transports sugars, chemicals, proteins, hormones, and many other substances around the body for use and elimination.

As the heart pumps blood, a pulse beat can be felt at various locations in the body, and each pulse beat corresponds to one heartbeat. The heart rate of the average adult at rest is between 60 to 100 beats per minute, depending on age, medical conditions and general fitness.

The respiratory system

This system is composed of the **airway** (mouth, nose, trachea, larynx, bronchi, and bronchioles) and the **lungs** (including the small air sacs called alveoli).

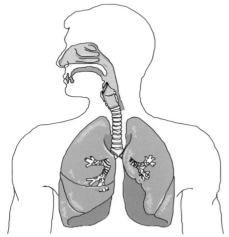

The respiratory system provides Oxygen to the blood, and takes away the waste product called Carbon Dioxide.

Oxygen is extracted from the air that is inhaled through the airway, and goes into the blood stream through the membranes of the lungs. For the first aider, maintaining a casualty's airway is of primary importance.

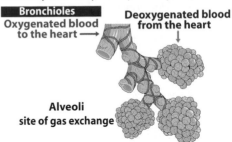

Bronchioles
Oxygenated blood to the heart →
Deoxygenated blood from the heart ↓
Alveoli site of gas exchange

The musculoskeletal system

This system involves the bones, ligaments, tendons and muscles which support the body, protect the internal organs, and enable movement.

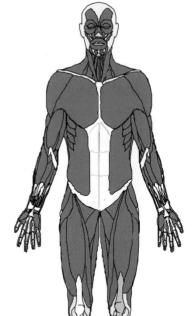

Most muscles used for movement work by contracting and relaxing in conjunction with a bone.

The action of raising your leg involves contracting several muscles, creating an opposing force in the leg, causing it to move upwards.

Some muscles, such as the *diaphragm* that makes the lungs expand and contract, do not need bones to work with, but function attached to large masses of tissue.

The digestive system

This system includes the oesophagus, stomach and intestines. Fluid and solids are passed through the oesophagus to the stomach where they are processed for further digestion. They are then absorbed into the body through the membranes of the intestines.

Some organs, such as the liver and pancreas, are considered accessories to the digestive system as they help process food into various chemical substances used by the body.

The endocrine system

This system involves those organs and glands that secrete chemicals in the form of **hormones** to stimulate and activate the body's functions.

The *pancreas* for example, controls a variety of important functions by releasing insulin, and influencing the body's metabolic process.

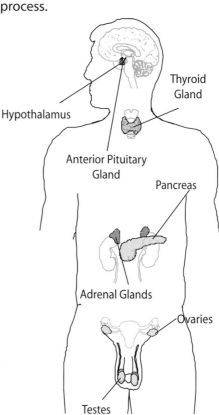

The urinary system

This is an important system that flushes waste products suspended in fluid from the body.

It includes the kidneys, bladder and urinary tract, and plays a vital role in keeping the body healthy.

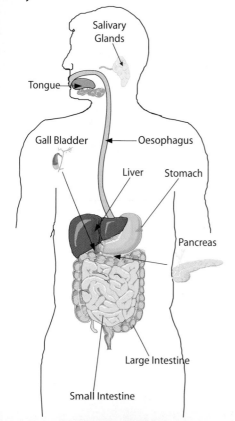

Should the urinary system fail (especially the kidneys), then the affected person requires external assistance to get rid of the waste products by 'flushing' the blood. This is called *haemodialysis* or, more commonly, '*dialysis*'.

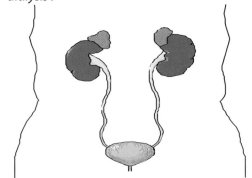

The reproductive system

This is linked to the body's **endocrine system**, through the female's *ovaries* and the male's *testes*. These are known as the *gonads*, or 'sex glands'.

The female reproductive system consists of the *ovaries* which produce the human egg, the *uterus* (or 'womb') where the fertilised egg is lodged for growth, and the *vagina*.

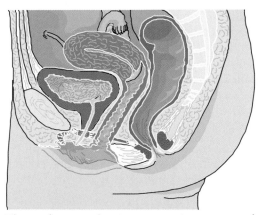

The male reproductive system is composed of the *testes*, which produce sperm, the *seminal vesicle* that provides the fluid medium for the sperm, and the *penis*.

The integumentary system

This is the system that includes **skin**, **hair**, **fingernails** and **toenails**. Their pigmentation (colour) and growth are linked to the *endocrine system*.

The skin is the body's largest organ, and plays an important role in protecting the body from infections. The skin's other functions include acting as a shield against injury and keeping body fluids in. The skin is made from tough, elastic fibres which have the ability to stretch without tearing easily.

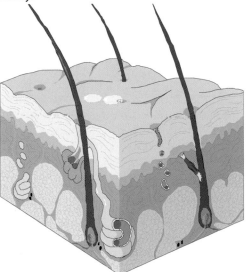

The lymphatic system

The lymphatic system is a slow moving system where toxins such as venom tend to accumulate after the bite has occurred.

This system provides lymphatic fluid that drains from the body's tissues, which is important as a 'flushing' mechanism, and most toxins and infections absorbed or injected into the tissues are collected by the lymphatic system and 'strained' through lymph nodes in the armpits, neck and groin. The lymphatic fluid eventually drains into the blood stream.

HYGIENE IN FIRST AID

Ensuring cleanliness in all first aid situations is extremely important. A first aider must take precautions to ensure that the risk of infection is minimised by practising good first aid hygiene procedures.

Infectious diseases are those diseases which cause infections to the human body, and in some cases are transmitted by contact or by cross-infection.

Infection may be due to bacteria, viruses, parasites or fungi.

The usual methods of communication are: **direct contact** (with an infected person); **indirect contact** (through coughing, air conditioning, or similar); or **through a host** (insects, worms).

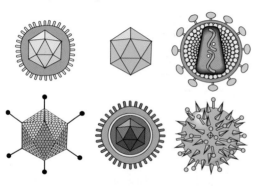

Many deadly infectious diseases have been eradicated, but several, such as poliomyelitis (a virus), are again on the increase. Many are preventable by immunisation. Some, such as *the Human Immunodeficiency Virus* (HIV), have no cure or immunisation as yet. Examples of infectious diseases are:

Viral Infections. *Measles, mumps, rubella, hepatitis, influenza, chickenpox, HIV and the common cold.*

Bacterial Infections. *Throat infections, whooping cough, diphtheria, rheumatic fever, tuberculosis strains, cholera, staphylococcus infection and some forms of meningitis.*

Parasitic Infections. *Malaria, tapeworm, hookworm, itch mites, pubic and body lice.*

Fungal Infections. *Ringworm, tinea ('Athlete's Foot') and thrush.*

The human body has natural defences against infection and remains immune to certain types. Immunity usually comes from surviving previous exposure with resultant antibodies being produced. The blood contains leucocytes (white blood cells), which help produce antibodies. The leucocytes and antibodies [try to] combat any infection which invades the body. Unfortunately, while the body responds quickly to infection, the initial defences can be overwhelmed if the infectious agent is numerous. When this happens the casualty develops the disease.

It is at this stage that the body requires help in the form of medically prescribed antibiotics or similar drugs.

General precautions

While there is little that the first aider can do to cure an infection there is a great deal that you can do to limit the risk of infection and treat the symptoms of minor infections. However, the first aid provider should be familiar with the signs and symptoms of the common diseases, and advise the infected person to seek appropriate medical attention.

Advice that the first aid provider can offer is:

- ✔ care of the susceptible, ie. the ill, the elderly, and the very young
- ✔ care in nutrition and preparation of food
- ✔ maintenance of personal hygiene
- ✔ maintenance of sanitary standards
- △ avoid direct contact with infection
- △ avoid transmitting infection

First aid hygiene

It is important that first aid procedures have due regard for the danger of cross-infection. Simple rules of personal hygiene and wearing gloves are sufficient to guard both the first aid provider and the casualty from contamination when treating or caring for a casualty.

PRIOR TO TREATMENT

- ✔ wash hands with soap and water, or rinse with antiseptic

- ✔ ensure that hands are washed thoroughly between fingers and under nails
- ✔ place a barrier between you and the casualty's body fluids

- ✔ always wear nitrile or latex gloves if available
- ✔ take care not to touch any unclean object when wearing gloves or once hands are washed
- ✔ if possible, use a protective cover over clothing
- ✔ cover any adjacent areas likely to produce infection

DURING TREATMENT

- ✔ use a face shield or mask with a one-way-valve or filter, if available, when performing resuscitation
- ✔ use only clean bandages and dressings
- △ avoid coughing, breathing, or speaking over the wound
- △ avoid contact with body fluids
- △ avoid treating more than one casualty without washing hands and changing gloves

AFTER TREATMENT

- ✔ clean up both casualty and yourself
- ✔ clean up the immediate vicinity
- ✔ dispose of dressings, bandages, sharps, gloves and soiled clothing safely and correctly
- ✔ wash hands with soap and water thoroughly, even if gloves were used

Waste materials can be placed inside a plastic bag, which is then placed inside another plastic bag and tied securely. Use a biohazard bag if possible. Do not place in rubbish bin. Seek advice from your local health department on disposal options.

Needle-Stick Injuries

The principal risk associated with needle stick injury is contracting blood borne viruses such as HIV (AIDS) and HBV (Hepatitis B).

There is a low risk of a person who is pricked or scratched by a discarded needle being infected with AIDS, Hepatitis B and Hepatitis C.

The most common sharps injuries are from needle-sticks, typically on the index finger and thumb. Needle-stick injuries account for up to 80% of all accidental exposures to blood.

Ways of reducing the risk of needlestick injuries include:

- ❐ It is generally recommended that workers who may come in contact with blood or body fluids should receive Hepatitis B vaccinations
- ❐ Follow all safety procedures in the workplace
- ❐ Latex or nitrile gloves will not protect you against needlestick injuries
- ❐ Never bend or snap used needles
- ❐ Never re-cap a needle
- ❐ Always place used needles into a clearly labelled and puncture-proof sharps approved container.

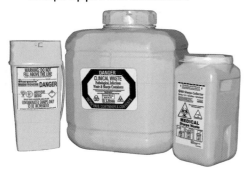

➕ CARE AND TREATMENT

- ✔ wash away the blood or body fluid with soap and water
- ✔ if the eyes are contaminated, rinse eyes while open with water or saline
- ✔ if blood gets into the mouth, spit it out and then repeatedly rinse with water

✔ refer the person immediately to a doctor or hospital emergency department who will assess the risk of transmission and discuss options for testing and treatment
✔ ensure the safe disposal of the sharp
✔ report the incident immediately.

Dispose of waste in accordance with the requirements of the relevant authorities.

EXAMINING A CASUALTY

Accurate casualty treatment, and later medical treatment, depends on accurate and detailed information from the incident scene.

At an incident it is important that you note as much information as you can. Details such as the estimated speed at which a car was moving, the way it hit an object, the size and shape of that object and whether the casualty was conscious or unconscious when you arrived.

Note all this and report it to the ambulance personnel or doctor. These are important details for emergency personnel trying to evaluate the casualty's injuries. You must approach the incident in a confident and methodical way. This not only allows you to gain information, but also presents you as someone who knows what they are doing. This attitude imparts confidence to the casualty and bystanders.

The approach

Take the time to look at the scene for anything that may threaten your safety or the safety of those on or around the scene.

Look for the number of casualties involved. Look for bystanders who may be able to supply information on what happened and the number of casualties.

What are your impressions as you approach the incident?

☐ Is it a road traffic accident?
☐ Has a person fallen from a ladder?

Quickly confirm in your mind just what is present; bystanders, other vehicles, power lines, power cables, or collapsed structures.

Primary examination

Check to see if the casualty is conscious. If unconscious treat as per the Emergency Action Plan.

Check to see if there is severe life threatening bleeding and control immediately.

Try to obtain a history from:

☐ The casualty
☐ Bystanders.

At this point you are able to decide what approach and treatment is appropriate.

If the casualty is conscious ask three important questions:

1. What happened?
2. Where does it hurt the most?
3. Can you take a deep breath?

These three questions will give you information from the casualty, including whether the casualty remembers the incident (were they unconscious), what injury hurts the most, and if any chest injuries may be affecting breathing.

Pay attention to:

History – the incident (**SAMPLE**)

☐ **S**igns and symptoms
☐ **A**llergies
☐ **M**edication
☐ **P**ast illnesses
☐ **L**ast time the casualty ate or drank
☐ **E**vent – history of injury/illness (what happened, where and when)

Signs – what you can see or feel for yourself

❏ Bleeding, swelling, bruising

Symptoms – what the casualty tells you

❏ Pain, blurred vision, nausea

Observations

One of the most important things a first aider can do is to take and record accurate observations. There are four vital observations that should be, if at all possible, written down against the time and the name of the casualty. These observations are:

❏ Skin appearance
❏ Conscious state
❏ Pulse
❏ Respiration

The first set of these observations, once taken and recorded, becomes the 'baseline observations'. All changes in the casualty's observations are measured against this baseline for improvement or worsening of their condition.

Skin Appearance

The appearance of the skin can be a good indicator of the casualty's condition. Check colour, condition and temperature of the skin.

Colour – always check the colour of skin in the mouth and lips. Red, pink, pale or blue. (Checking the lining of the mouth and lips allows a quick assessment of casualties from all ethnic backgrounds).

Temperature – is the skin warm or cool to touch?

Condition – is the skin dry or wet?

Conscious State

Check the casualty for a response by touching the casualty on the shoulders and asking loudly *'are you all right'*?

Note the following:

❏ Is the casualty alert and aware of time and place?
❏ Is the casualty confused, violent or agitated?
❏ Is the casualty roused by touch or pain?

There are 4 levels of consciousness (**AVPU**).

1. **A**lert – the casualty is responsive and alert and aware of time and place.
2. Responsive to **V**erbal stimulus – the casualty is not aware of time and place.
3. The casualty responds only to **P**ainful stimuli.
3. **U**nresponsive – the casualty does not respond to stimuli.

Pulse

The pulse can be difficult to find and **should only be used** when time permits and when assessing a casualty that is breathing. **DO NOT** use a pulse to determine if resuscitation is required.

The neck is the best location to check for a pulse, which is called the carotid. The carotid is the strongest and most easily accessible of all the pulse points. The radial pulse (wrist) is often the easiest to find. When taking a pulse, note how fast the pulse rate is over one minute. A normal adult will have a pulse rate of 60 to 100 beats per minute. Children and babies have a faster heart rate than adults. Note the rate, rhythm and strength of the pulse.

- ❐ **Rate** – How many beats per minute? Count for 15 seconds and multiply by 4
  - ⊃ Adults – 60 to 100 beats per minute
  - ⊃ Children – 90 to 130 beats per minute
  - ⊃ Infants – 120 to 160 beats per minute
- ❐ **Rhythm** – Is the pulse regular or irregular?
- ❐ **Strength** – Is the pulse strong or weak?

RESPIRATION

- ❐ Rate – How many breaths per minute? Count for 15 seconds and multiply by 4
- ❐ Rhythm – Is the breathing regular or irregular?
- ❐ Sounds – Is there gasping, gurgling, wheezing or snoring?

PAIN

Pain can be one of the most difficult observations to make as every person has a different '*pain threshold*'. Ask **open questions** such as *"can you describe your pain to me"*, not *"does your pain feel sharp"*.

As pain is subjective the first aider needs to use a tool such as the **PQRST** of pain.

Provocation – What brought the pain on? Did the pain start when the casualty was at rest or did it start with activity or injury?

Quality – How is the pain described? Is it intermittent, sharp, dull, heavy, burning or an ache?

Region/**R**adiation – Where is the pain situated, and does it travel to other areas of the body?

Severity – Measure the pain on a scale of 1 to 10. A rating of 10 on this scale would be severe pain.

Time – How long ago did the pain start?

Secondary examination

Now that you know the casualty's basic observations and condition you have more time to thoroughly examine a conscious casualty by systematically *Looking and Feeling* (**LAF**).

- ❐ **L**ook for deformity, wounds and swelling
- ❐ **A**nd
- ❐ **F**eel for deformity, tenderness and swelling

A good tool to remember the signs of injury is **DOTS**.

- ❐ **D**eformity
- ❐ **O**pen wounds
- ❐ **T**enderness
- ❐ **S**welling

Conduct a head-to-toes *secondary examination*. *Remember to be sensitive to the **age, sex and culture** of the casualty.*

Start the secondary examination by informing the casualty of what you are going to do and the reason for doing the examination. Listen carefully to what the casualty tells you while doing your examination.

HEAD:
- ❏ Bleeding
- ❏ Fractures
- ❏ Bruising
- ❏ Swelling
- ❏ Tenderness or pain
- ❏ Cerebral spinal fluid (CSF) from ears. CSF is a clear colourless fluid that may also have evidence of blood mixed with it
- ❏ Ask casualty to bite to check for fractured jaw

NECK:
- ❏ Bleeding
- ❏ Fractures
- ❏ Bruising
- ❏ Swelling
- ❏ Deformity
- ❏ Tenderness or pain
- ❏ Numbness or tingling
- ❏ Check for Medical Alert necklace
- ❏ Ask casualty to wiggle fingers and toes
- ❏ Ask casualty to squeeze your hands to check for strength

SHOULDERS AND CHEST:
- ❏ Bruising
- ❏ Swelling
- ❏ Gently 'spring' the ribs to check for tenderness or pain
- ❏ Look for unequal rise of the chest with each breath
- ❏ abdomen and pelvis:

- ❏ Rigidity
- ❏ Tenderness or pain
- ❏ Swelling
- ❏ 'Guarding' and incontinence
- ❏ Gently 'spring' the pelvis to check for tenderness or pain

ARMS AND LEGS:
- ❏ Bleeding
- ❏ Fractures
- ❏ Soft tissue injuries
- ❏ Tenderness or pain
- ❏ Loss of strength
- ❏ Check for medical alert bracelet
- ❏ Check circulation in extremities
- ❏ Ask casualty to move each limb in turn

BACK AND SPINE:
- ❏ Bleeding
- ❏ Deformity
- ❏ Tenderness or pain
- ❏ 'Log roll' and look at all areas of the back of the casualty for signs of injury

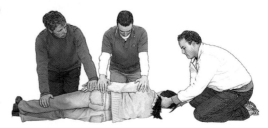

ROAD TRAFFIC ACCIDENTS

Most modern vehicles are designed to withstand impacts of a certain force, and to provide protection to drivers and passengers. Seat belts, 'crumple zones', collapsible steering wheels, airbags, roll bars – all these and similar devices are designed to provide personal protection in an accident. Unfortunately, not all vehicles on the road are equipped with these modern design benefits, and many provide little or no protection at all.

As a first aid provider, you may be required to render assistance at the scene of a road traffic accident. If so, remember, be calm and methodical in your actions as others involved who have not had the benefit of first aid training will look to you for support and guidance – for leadership.

Approaching the scene

Consider your safety and that of bystanders and the casualty. Always take time to have a good look at the scene before you approach. Approach the scene methodically, keep away from traffic, and ask someone to accompany you as an assistant.

Examine the scene – give yourself time to think about your next action.

There are many things to consider, including:

- ❏ Is the vehicle stable; will it roll or move?
- ❏ Is there spilt fuel?

- ❏ Is there any risk of fire?
- ❏ Are power poles involved?
- ❏ What about oncoming traffic?
- ❏ If a van or truck; is the load safe?
- ❏ **DO NOT** touch anything until you are sure that it is safe.

Controlling the scene

As you move to the scene, ask bystanders to move back. Ask a responsible person to slow down or redirect any oncoming traffic (ask if anyone has a torch). Ask someone else to make sure that bystanders (especially children) don't become involved with passing traffic. Ask bystanders not to smoke near any damaged vehicles.

Unless there is someone else present with more advanced medical knowledge, you become the person in charge of the casualties.

Assess the scene

What are your initial impressions.

- ❏ How many casualties?
- ❏ Are they walking around?

- ❏ Unconscious?
- ❏ Talking?
- ❏ Any obviously dead?
- ❏ Any trapped?
- ❏ Immobile?

After the initial quick assessment, ask the person who accompanied you to contact the ambulance service and give them information on location, number of casualties, estimated seriousness of injuries, and if road rescue is required for trapped casualties.

Ask bystanders for help; 'Are there any first aiders here?', 'Did anyone see what happened?' 'Could someone give me a hand?' It is at this point that you may be required to *triage* the casualties (*refer to Triage on page 26*) – remember, first aid is provided to the casualties who will benefit most, eg the unconscious, the person bleeding profusely.

Without adequate help, do not become committed to resuscitating a cardiac arrest casualty at the expense of others who require urgent assistance.

Access to the casualties

Ensure that any vehicle involved is safe. Do not touch the vehicle unless you are certain it is safe to do so. Check the vehicle is not in contact with an electrical power source.

If you attempt to gain entry, do not wrench open the door unless you know that it is not in contact with a casualty. In certain circumstances, casualties have become impaled or entrapped by contact with a door.

Be careful of broken glass if you insert your head through a window. Make sure that you can gain effective entry beside and behind the casualty. Beware of sharp metal and broken glass.

Attending the casualties

Perform a primary examination of the casualties. Use any helpers to move the casualties with minor injuries ('walking wounded') away from the scene to a safe place. This will give you more room to attend to the more serious cases.

Always try to have a responsible person to help you attend to serious casualties – it helps to have assistance and support.

What to look for

Always consider the outcomes of the accident: Was the vehicle struck on the side ('T-boned')? Did it roll over? Was it a high-speed impact? Was the motorcyclist hit by his own bike? There are certain injuries that appear associated with particular types of impact ('mechanism of injury'), and considering the accident's effects may point you towards any suspected, but perhaps less visible, injuries:

Side impact. Fractured upper leg (femur) and/or lower leg on the side of impact. Consider a fractured pelvis. Suspect a shoulder or upper arm injury on the side of impact, and if the 'B' pillar has been damaged, suspect a head injury.

High speed impact. Deceleration injuries involving severe internal bleeding, multiple fractures, impacted pelvis, head and spinal injuries, and multiple lacerations. Be alert for deterioration in unconscious casualties with head injuries.

Rear end collisions. Cervical spine injuries ('whiplash' effect) and facial injuries.

Ejection from the vehicle. Head and spinal injuries, unconsciousness, multiple fractures, multiple lacerations to upper body and head, and internal bleeding.

Roll over. This mechanism of injury provides for the complete range of damage to the human body.

Drivers and passengers are usually thrown around, irrespective of their seat belt restraints, and they have no control over their movements.

Pay particular attention to children, as they are often not correctly restrained by seatbelts designed for adults.

Motorcycle accidents. Injuries commonly sustained by riders and pillion passengers are fractures of the femur, wrist and ankle fractures, head injuries, and deceleration injuries resulting in severe internal bleeding.

Motor cyclists' helmets **should not** be removed unless the airway is obstructed or the casualty is not breathing.

Casualties should remove their own helmets wherever possible. If a helmet has to be removed, it requires two rescuers to do so, and it should be done carefully with no movement of the neck.

Bicycle accidents. Cyclists are liable to sustain multiple fractures, multiple lacerations, and head injuries. Children are susceptible to 'greenstick' fractures of the arms, and wrist injuries through falling off at relatively low speed.

Pedestrians. Generally, adults are struck on their side as they try to turn away from the vehicle. Their injuries are usually more pronounced on the side that has received the impact.

Children and the elderly are more likely to be struck as they turn to face the oncoming vehicle.

Most pedestrians are 'run under' rather than 'run over' as they are forced off their feet by the impact and may be thrown over the vehicle, or for some distance from the point of impact. Head and spinal injuries are common, especially where the casualty's head has struck the vehicle's bonnet or windscreen. Small children may be 'run over', and be still under the vehicle when it stops.

Treatment of casualties

Treat any casualties in accordance with your training. **DO NOT** remove any seriously injured casualties from the vehicle unless fire, fear of further collision, airway protection, control of severe bleeding, or CPR are necessary.

Wait for the ambulance to arrive. Provide what treatment and reassurance you can, keep the casualties warm with blankets if available, and periodically check on the 'walking wounded' who have been moved from the scene.

Remember that *shock* is a life-threatening condition, and may be present after trauma sustained in a road traffic accident. Be ready to treat any signs and symptoms that indicate a casualty is progressing into shock.

Do not confuse shock with the adrenaline 'rush' associated with the 'fight or flight' mechanism which causes people involved to shiver, shake, cry and feel faint after an accident. This is not a serious condition, and others can look after them while you attend to the needy casualties.

On arrival of the ambulance, give the crew what information you have and advise them of any treatment you have provided. Your intervention will be appreciated by all concerned – especially the casualties.

MULTIPLE CASUALTIES

Triage (*pronounced 'tree-ahz'*), is a French word used in the first aid and medical contexts to indicate the sorting and classification of casualties, and the establishment of treatment priorities. It usually refers to a mass casualty situation, such as an earthquake or bus accident.

Even though triage generally applies to large numbers of casualties, it is also relevant to other first aid situations involving two or more casualties.

There are times when members of the public, trained in first aid, have had to make decisions on the treatment and care of casualties which normally would have been the responsibility of ambulance officers or a doctor. This is especially relevant in country areas where medical aid may be some time away. A common example of this circumstance is when a member of the public travelling a remote country road comes across a motor vehicle accident involving several casualties.

Unfortunately, to effectively provide the best treatment for the most needy, some seriously injured casualties may have to be temporarily ignored. Basically, the requirement is for your limited first aid resources to be allocated to the casualties who will survive because of it, and not to those who are likely to die.

To triage an incident, your approach has to be objective. To assume the responsibility for these decisions is an unenviable position to be in.

You should ask yourself three questions:

1. Who needs immediate treatment to save their life?
2. Who will really benefit, and who won't?
3. If I treat one person, will others suffer seriously from lack of attention?

Safety, airway, breathing, circulation, control of severe bleeding, shock, and burns, are still the priorities when attending multiple casualties with little, or no assistance.

Casualties in cardiac arrest are only given CPR if there are no other seriously injured casualties requiring life-saving treatment. If you become distracted with a casualty in cardiac arrest, you will be fully committed performing CPR (usually to no avail), at the expense of another who may be saved by your active intervention.

An unconscious casualty on their back, a person with severe bleeding, a casualty with a head injury going into shock – all are high priorities because without your intervention they may die. A conscious casualty with a fractured leg is less urgent and can wait until the more serious casualties are dealt with. A conscious casualty walking around, complaining of a sore shoulder, for example, is at the bottom of the triage list.

The most knowledgeable or experienced person present should undertake triage.

THE CHAIN OF SURVIVAL

It is estimated that more than 95% of sudden cardiac arrest casualties die before reaching a hospital. However, when all four links of the Chain of Survival are strong, survival rates for casualties of Sudden Cardiac Arrest (SCA) can rise to as high as 40%. By understanding more about sudden cardiac arrest and the importance of the Chain of Survival concept, you may be able to save the life of a family member, a neighbour, co-worker or a friend.

The four links in the Chain of Survival are:

1st Link – Early Recognition and Call for Help

The first link shows the importance of the early recognition of those at risk of cardiac arrest and then calling for help immediately in the hope that early treatment can prevent cardiac arrest.

2nd Link – Early CPR

Early Cardiopulmonary Resuscitation (CPR) performed by a first aider on a casualty who is in cardiac arrest can buy life-saving time.

3rd Link – Early Defibrillation

Early defibrillation is the third and perhaps most significant link. Automated External Defibrillation is the emergency procedure where specially trained first aiders apply an electronic device to the chest of a cardiac arrest casualty, and the device automatically delivers a controlled electric shock to the casualty's heart.

4th Link – Early ACLS

Advanced Cardiac Life Support is provided by ambulance paramedics and other highly trained medical personnel. Effective post resuscitation care is mainly aimed at preserving brain and heart function.

FIRST AID KITS

You may hope that an emergency never occurs, but if it does you need to be prepared. Part of being prepared is keeping an appropriately stocked and maintained first aid kit. Having an adequate first aid kit equips you to provide emergency assistance if required.

Keep a first aid kit at home, in your car and at your workplace. The best first aid kits take into account the specific uses the kit is designed for.

Store first aid kits in a cool, clean and dry location that is childproof. A regular check of contents is essential, ensuring the contents are present, not out of date and are in good condition.

Make sure that all your family members and staff know where the first aid kit is so that it can be quickly retrieved in an emergency.

Under the Health and Safety (First-Aid) Regulations 1981 and Approved Code of Practice and Guidance, L74 1997, at least one first aid kit must be kept in any workplace.

Sufficient back up stock should be kept on hand. All first aid kits must be identified by a white cross on a green background.

The contents of first aid kits in the workplace is not mandated, and the contents should be determined based on a risk assessment using the HSE *assessment of first aid needs*.

If you require more information on first aid kits, speak to your local first aid provider.

A suggested list of contents

Sterile adhesive dressings (assorted sizes) to suit workplace	20
First Aid Leaflet giving general guidance	1
Triangular Bandage (preferably sterile)	4
Medium Sterile Unmedicated Wound Dressings (12 cm x 12 cm)	6
Large Sterile Unmedicated Wound Dressings (18 cm x 18 cm)	2
Gloves Disposable	2
Safety Pins	6
Sterile Eye Pads	2

The above is a suggested list of contents, where there is no special risk in the workplace, provided by the HSE. Equivalent but different items will be considered acceptable.

Typically there are three generally available first aid kits for the workplace covering up to 10, 20 and 50 people. These are commonly referred to as 'HSE kits'.

Useful Resources

Health & Safety Executive (HSE)
  http://www.hse.gov.uk/firstaid
Reporting of Injuries, Diseases and Dangerous Occurrences Regulations
  http://www.riddor.gov.uk
  ☎ 0845 3009923
First Aid Cafe
  http://www.firstaidcafe.co.uk

- ✍ The Basic Life Support Flow Chart
- ✍ The emergency action plan
- ✍ The unconscious casualty
- ✍ Managing an airway
- ✍ Rescue Breaths
- ✍ Cardiopulmonary Resuscitation (CPR)

Quick and effective management of an emergency requires a plan of action. This section provides you with the most widely accepted plan for handling first aid emergencies, and covers each essential step of the action plan in detail.

By the end of this section you should be able to:
- ✚ Follow the steps in the Basic Life Support Flow Chart.
- ✚ List the five steps in the Emergency Action Plan.
- ✚ Demonstrate the management of an unconscious casualty.
- ✚ Recognise and clear an obstructed airway.
- ✚ Perform rescue breaths on all age groups.
- ✚ Perform compressions on all age groups.
- ✚ Perform CPR on all age groups.

BASIC LIFE SUPPORT FLOW CHART

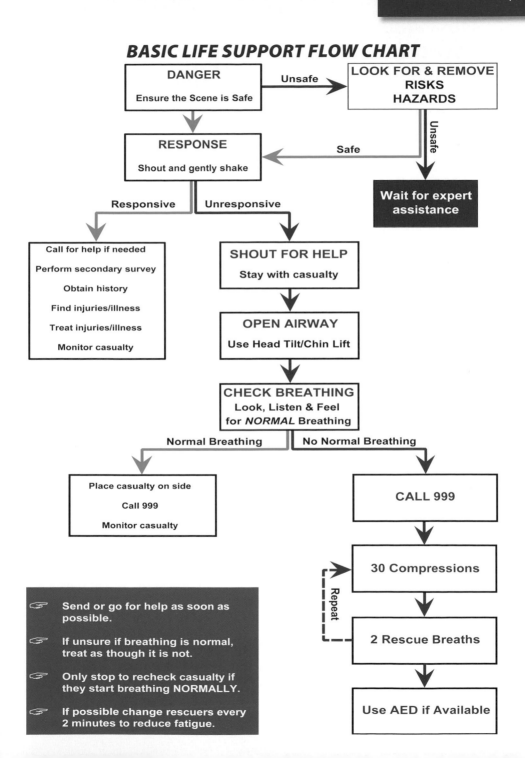

EMERGENCY ACTION PLAN

The emergency action plan consists of five steps, **Danger** (Safety), **Response**, **Airway**, **Breathing**, **Compressions and Defibrillation**.

These steps are known as **DRABCD** and are the major consideration for everyone involved in the care and treatment of casualties.

Danger

Once an emergency has occurred you need to ensure the safety of all those at the scene by checking for hazards. Check for any risk to:

❑ Yourself   ❑ Bystanders   ❑ Casualties

Take the time to conduct a primary survey of the scene to look for anything that may threaten the safety of those on or around the scene.

Hazards that may be present include:

△ bio-hazards	△ fallen power lines
△ bombs	△ falling masonry
△ bullets	△ fast flowing water
△ chemicals	△ flammable material
△ electricity	△ on coming traffic
△ fire	△ risk of explosion
△ fumes	△ sharp metal edges
△ gases	△ slippery surfaces
△ smoke	△ unstable structures

Leave dangerous situations to the emergency personnel who have the training and equipment to manage the situation. Risking your own safety in a dangerous situation may increase the number of casualties to manage.

Other situations may permit the removal of the hazard, or the removal of the casualty from the hazard. Examples of removing a hazard would be cleaning away broken glass at a motor vehicle accident scene, or turning electricity off at the main powerboard in an electrocution incident.

As a general rule you should avoid moving casualties unless there is a hazard that you cannot remove, such as fire or poisonous fumes. Moving a casualty, especially an unconscious casualty, is very difficult and should be left to ambulance personnel who have the training and equipment necessary to protect themselves and the casualty.

If it is essential to move a casualty before an ambulance arrives, take extreme care and use good manual handling practice.

Provided they are not at further risk, you should check casualties in the position in which you find them.

In the event that you are unable to check a casualty in the position that they are in, gently roll them onto their back, supporting the head and neck during movement.

Response

Check the casualty for a response by *gently* shaking the casualty's shoulders and asking loudly *'are you all right?'*.

DO NOT shake children and infants, and there is no need to aggressively shake a casualty to gain a response, just gently shaking the casualty on the shoulders and talking loudly is an effective method and will awaken a sleeping person. A casualty that is unresponsive should be considered unconscious.

IF THE CASUALTY RESPONDS

If the casualty responds by answering and appears conscious, leave them in the position in which you find them (provided they are not at further risk).

- ✔ check the casualty's condition and send or go for help, or call 999 for an ambulance if required
  - ☛ if you are on your own, leave the casualty and go for help
- ✔ observe and reassess the casualty's regularly

IF THE CASUALTY DOES NOT RESPOND

- ✔ shout for help
- ✔ roll the casualty onto their back
- ✔ check airway

Airway

Ensuring an open airway is essential.

Open Airway

- ✔ place your hand on the forehead and gently tilt the head back
- ✔ place your fingertips under the point of the casualty's chin and lift the chin to open the airway.
  - ☛ in children and infants do not press on the soft tissues under the chin as this may block the airway
- ✔ check breathing

ⓘ *Try to avoid head tilt if injury to the neck is suspected. If neck injury is suspected use chin lift to open the airway.*

Breathing

Keep the airway open and check for *normal breathing*.

- ✔ *look, listen* and *feel* for **no more** than 10 seconds for normal breathing
  - ☛ **look** to see if the chest rises
  - ☛ **listen** for the sound of normal breathing
  - ☛ **feel** for air against your cheek

In the first few minutes of a casualty's cardiac arrest, sounds of gurgling, sighing or coughing may be present, as well as movements of the chest and stomach. This type of breathing is ineffective, as it does not move air into or out of the lungs and the casualty should be treated as if they are not breathing.

ⓘ *If you are in any doubt that the casualty is breathing normally, treat as if they are not breathing.*

If Breathing Present

✔ roll into recovery position
✔ check the casualty's condition and get help if needed
✔ observe and reassess the casualty for continued breathing regularly

If Breathing Absent

✔ send or go for help, or call **'999'** for an ambulance
   ☛ if you are on your own, leave the casualty and go for help
✔ send someone for the AED
✔ start chest compressions

Compressions

If the casualty is unresponsive and not breathing normally commence compressions.

✔ kneel by the side of the casualty
✔ place your hands, or two fingers with an infant, in the centre of the casualty's chest interlocking your fingers
✔ press straight down on the sternum 100 times per minute (a little less than 2 compressions a second)
✔ give 30 compressions
   ☛ *adults* - compress 4 – 5 cm
   ☛ *children/infants* - compress $\frac{1}{3}$ chest depth
✔ give 2 breaths
   ☛ open the airway
   ☛ close the casualty's nose
   ☛ blow into the casualty's mouth for about 1 second
   ☛ watch for chest rise with each breath

   ☛ give second breath
✔ return your hands or fingers quickly to the centre of the casualty's chest and then give the next compressions and breaths
✔ continue 30 compressions and 2 breaths cycles
✔ apply Automated External Defibrillator (AED) if available

△ **DO NOT** apply any pressure over the casualty's ribs, upper abdomen or the bottom end of the bony sternum (breastbone)

Defibrillation

Defibrillation is the emergency procedure where first aiders apply an electronic device called an Automated External Defibrillator or AED to the chest of a cardiac arrest casualty and the device delivers a controlled electric shock to the casualty's heart.

✔ send someone for the AED if not already done
✔ ensure safety
  ☞ If multiple rescuers are present, assign tasks for each rescuer
✔ turn on the AED
✔ attach the electrode pads
  ☞ if multiple rescuers, continue CPR while the pads are attached
✔ follow the voice/visual prompts of the AED
✔ ensure that nobody touches the casualty while the AED is analysing the rhythm

If a shock is indicated:

✔ ensure that nobody touches the casualty

✔ push the shock button as directed.
  ☞ fully-automatic AEDs will deliver the shock automatically
✔ continue to follow the voice/visual prompts of the AED

If no shock is indicated:

✔ immediately resume CPR using a ratio of 30 compressions to 2 rescue breaths.
✔ continue to follow the voice/visual prompts of the AED

Unsuccessful rescue breaths

If rescue breaths do not make the chest rise with each attempt, give 30 compressions and then before your next attempt at rescue breaths:

✔ check the casualty's mouth and remove any visible obstructions
✔ ensure that there is adequate head tilt and chin lift
△ **DO NOT** attempt more than two rescue breaths each time before returning to chest compressions

Chest compression only CPR

If for any reason rescue breaths can not be given, chest compressions should still be administered as some oxygen will still be circulated. Compress in the centre of the casualty's chest continuously 100 times per minute.

Re-checking for circulation

You should only stop to re-check the casualty if they start breathing normally again, otherwise do not interrupt resuscitation.

Multiple rescuers

If there is more than one rescuer present, change over the roll of performing CPR approximately every 2 minutes to reduce fatigue. Change over with minimal delay between compressions.

When to stop CPR

❒ The scene becomes unsafe

❒ Qualified help arrives and takes over

❒ The casualty shows signs of recovery

❒ You become physically unable to continue

When to get help

❒ If more than one rescuer is available, one should start resuscitation while another rescuer goes for assistance

❒ In children or infants if only one rescuer is available, then perform 1 minute of CPR before leaving to go for assistance

❒ If the casualty is an infant or small child it may be possible to take them with you

❒ If the collapse was sudden, not caused by trauma or poisoning and the casualty is a child with a history of heart disease, go for help immediately

Useful Resource

Resuscitation Council UK
http://www.resus.org.uk

THE UNCONSCIOUS CASUALTY

When breathing has been restored, it is essential to maintain the airway and ensure that the tongue, fluids or other objects do not cause an obstruction. It is also important to reduce the risk of inhalation of stomach contents.

Any unconscious casualty who remains on their back risks an obstructed airway through either inhaling vomitus, or by having their upper airway blocked by a relaxed tongue.

The most effective way of controlling this problem is to put the unconscious breathing casualty in a position that ensures the airway remains open by draining away any vomitus, or by allowing the relaxed tongue to move away from the airway opening. This position is called the recovery position, also known as the 'coma' or 'lateral' position.

This position places the casualty on their side, with the head down and tilted in such a way which expels any vomitus onto the ground, and the tongue falls clear of the airway opening.

 To prevent distress to the foetus, place women in advanced pregnancy on the left side unless prevented by injuries.

PROCEDURE FOR PLACING A CASUALTY IN THE RECOVERY POSITION

✔ prepare the casualty by checking pockets and removing items such as keys, and spectacles

✔ kneel beside the casualty and make sure that both their legs are straight

✔ place the arm nearest to you out at right angles (90°) to the body

- ✔ bring the farthest arm from you across the chest, and place the back of the hand under the casualty's cheek
- ✔ using your other hand, grasp the farthest leg just above the knee and pull it up, ensuring the foot stays on the ground
- ✔ keeping the hand under the casualty's cheek, pull the leg towards you to roll the casualty onto their side
- ✔ adjust the upper leg so that both the hip and knee are bent at right angles
- ✔ tilt the head back to make sure the airway remains open
- ✔ adjust the hand under the cheek to keep the head tilted
- ✔ check the casualty's breathing regularly

ℹ️ *If the casualty is to remain in the recovery position for any more than 30 minutes, turn them over to the other side if injuries permit.*

AIRWAY MANAGEMENT

Unconscious casualties have no control over their muscles, including the muscles that control the tongue.

Airway Open

Airway Closed

Airway Obstructed

The relaxed tongue will fall backwards and block the airway. If a breathing, unconscious casualty remains on their back, the risk of airway obstruction increases.

By tilting the head back and lifting the chin forward, the tongue is pulled away from the back of the throat. Ensuring a clear airway is essential so the casualty can breathe.

Material in the mouth (such as food, blood or vomitus) may also obstruct the airway of an unconscious casualty. It is vital that if such material is present it is removed.

In some cases the casualty may regurgitate or vomit the stomach contents which then enter the mouth and nose causing an obstruction. Regurgitation is more likely if the casualty is not provided with correct head tilt and chin lift.

There are 2 types of head tilt used in resuscitation:

- ❑ **Neutral** – used for infants and with suspected spinal injury casualties
- ❑ **Backward** – used in resuscitation of older children and adults

By combining correct head tilt and effective chin lift, you can assist the casualty to have an open and clear airway and reduce the risk of regurgitation.

In most situations, the airway can be managed with the use of head tilt and chin lift. If the airway is obstructed by a foreign body or fluid, then the airway should be cleared with the casualty lying on their side to avoid accidental inhalation of obstructions.

- ❑ Unless you can fully assess a casualty in the position in which you find them, turn the casualty onto their back
- ❑ Place your hand on the forehead and gently tilt the head back
- ❑ Support and lift the chin to open the airway
- ❑ Remove dislodged or loose dentures
- ❑ Leave well fitting dentures in place

A casualty requiring rescue breaths depends on an open airway.

If rescue breaths are unsuccessful you will need to clear the airway after the next cycle of compressions.

- ❑ Remove any visible obstruction from the casualty's mouth

The airways of an *infant* or *young child* are kept open and clear by supporting the head in the horizontal (neutral) position. **DO NOT** extend the head backwards.

If opening the airway is difficult in the horizontal position, tilt the infant or child's head back slightly with a gentle movement until the airway opens.

Backward head tilt

This method is used for a casualty in the side position, or when on their back before starting rescue breaths or CPR.

✔ place your hand on the forehead and gently tilt the head back

✔ place your fingertips under the point of the casualty's chin and lift the chin to open the airway.

    ☛ in children and infants do not press on the soft tissues under the chin as this may block the airway

Jaw thrust

In some instances involving injuries or illness, the casualty's airway may be difficult to open. An alternative method of airway maintenance is the jaw thrust.

❑ **Apply** pressure with the fingers behind the angle of the jaw

❑ **Thrust** the jaw gently forward and up, opening the airway

Clearing the airway of an upright casualty

In some instances, a casualty is trapped or held in a position which prevents the first aider placing them flat on the ground. It still remains vital the airway is kept clear. The best way to do this is applying backward head tilt and chin lift.

Great care is needed if there is any possibility of a spinal injury given the entire weight of the casualty's head may need supporting. Once backward head tilt is applied, keep the head in that position and do not allow it to fall forward again.

CHOKING

Choking follows the lodgement of a foreign object in the casualty's airway. In some instances, the object lodges at the epiglottis, the entry to the airway, but does not actually enter the airway itself. Both situations cause initial coughing, which is the body's reflex action to dislodge the object

If an object is firmly lodged in the airway, coughing at least keeps it high in the trachea, though may not expel it. However, coughing with an object at the entrance to the airway will generally cause it to be expelled.

Should you encounter a person with an apparent obstruction who is *coughing effectively*, **DO NOT SLAP** them on the back. If the obstruction is at the entrance to the trachea, then reactions to the slaps may cause the person to inhale the object and cause complete obstruction.

If a casualty appears to be in increasing distress, then the object may be totally obstructing the airway.

PARTIAL OBSTRUCTION

 SIGNS AND SYMPTOMS

○ difficulty in breathing

○ wheezing

○ snoring sound

○ persistent cough

○ cyanosis (blue skin colour)

○ in children and infants

    ➲ flaring of the nostrils

    ➲ in-drawing of the tissues above the sternum and in between the ribs

CARE AND TREATMENT

✔ encourage the casualty to keep coughing, but do nothing else.
① if blockage has not been cleared call **'999'** for an ambulance
✔ reassurance
△ **DO NOT** slap the casualty with a partial obstruction on the back

COMPLETE OBSTRUCTION

 SIGNS AND SYMPTOMS

○ unable to breathe, speak or cough
○ agitated and distressed
○ may grip the throat
○ bluish skin colour
○ rapid loss of consciousness

CARE AND TREATMENT

Conscious casualty

✔ position yourself to deliver back blows
  ☞ **adult**
    ☞ stand slightly behind and to the side of the casualty
    ☞ support the chest with one hand
    ☞ lean the casualty well forward
  ☞ **child**
    ☞ lean the casualty over your arm and hold them forwards so that the head is lower than the chest
  ☞ **baby**
    ☞ lay the casualty over your arm face down and bend them forwards so that the head is lower than the chest

✔ deliver up to five firm back blows between the shoulder blades using the heel of the hand
✔ check mouth and clear any obstructions that may have come loose after each back blow

✔ if back blows are unsuccessful deliver up to five abdominal thrusts
✔ stand or knee behind the casualty
  ☞ **adult and child**
    ☞ place both arms round the upper part of the abdomen
    ☞ lean the casualty forward
    ☞ clench your fist and place it between the umbilicus (navel) and the bottom end of the sternum (breastbone)
    ☞ grasp the fist with your other hand and pull sharply inwards and upwards
△ **DO NOT** give abdominal thrusts to babies, use chest thrusts instead
  ☞ **baby**
    ☞ lay the baby face up over your arm with head slightly down
    ☞ give up to 5 chest thrusts. Chest thrusts are similar to chest compressions only slower and sharper
✔ check mouth and clear any obstructions that may have come loose after each back blow
✔ if the obstruction is still not relieved, continue alternating five back blows with five abdominal thrusts

Unconscious casualty

✔ support the casualty carefully to the ground
① call **'999'** for an ambulance
✔ commence CPR

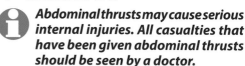 *Abdominal thrusts may cause serious internal injuries. All casualties that have been given abdominal thrusts should be seen by a doctor.*

 After removal of the object a casualty with a persistent cough, difficulty swallowing, or with the sensation of an object being still stuck in the throat should be seen by a doctor.

RESCUE BREATHING

On breathing in (inspiration), a person inspires approximately 21% oxygen, and the body uses between 4-5% of this amount for its normal functions. Therefore when a person breathes out (expiration) they expire approximately 16% of oxygen.

To breathe into another person as a means of supplementing their oxygen supply is essential for a non-breathing casualty. Immediate rescue breaths are necessary! If the brain is deprived of oxygen it begins to suffer irreversible tissue damage in 3-4 minutes.

Rescue breaths are necessary for casualties who are nor breathing. Certain conditions cause the loss of breathing and the first aider should assess the need for resuscitation. Choking, heroin overdose, near drowning, certain bites and stings, as well as respiratory conditions such as asthma and emphysema can cause respiratory arrest necessitating rapid and effective rescue breaths to sustain life.

Rescue Breathing is the method by which a rescuer breathes for a casualty who is not breathing.

The common term is *'mouth-to-mouth resuscitation'*. It is an effective method for buying time, as a rescuer breathes out sufficient oxygen to supply a casualty until more advanced help arrives.

There are five main methods of delivering rescue breaths:

Mouth-to-Mouth is where the rescuer seals the casualty's mouth with their own mouth, pinches the nose closed, and then blows air into the casualty's mouth.

Mouth-to-Nose is used where the casualty has sustained facial injuries that preclude using the mouth. The rescuer closes the casualty's mouth, covers the nose with their mouth, breathes gently, and then releases the casualty's jaw to allow exhalation.

Mouth-to-Nose-&-Mouth is the preferred method when resuscitating an infant or young child, as the rescuer's mouth can cover and seal the nose and mouth.

Mouth-to-Stoma is used for resuscitating a casualty who breathes through a stoma, an opening in the neck, through which the casualty normally breathes. The rescuer breathes through the stoma directly into the airway while blocking the nose and mouth. Casualties who have a stoma often wear a scarf or fabric filter over the stoma. Be alert for the presence of a stoma under such wrappings.

Mouth-to-Mask is the most desirable method for rescue breaths as it lessens the risk of cross-infection and is more acceptable to many people than mouth-to-mouth. Masks come in various forms but they are used in a similar way

The mask is fitted firmly over the casualty's nose and mouth and the rescuer delivers rescue breaths via the valve or tube thus avoiding direct contact with the casualty's mouth or expired air.

Rescue breaths must be effective, and are considered effective if the chest rises and falls with each breath given by the rescuer.

When considering which resuscitation technique to use, take account of the age of the casualty. The age groups are:

❐ Infant – Under 1 year
❐ Child – Between 1 year and puberty
❐ Adult – Puberty and older

If the rescuer believes the casualty to be a child treat as for a child.

Each breath should take 1 second. When breathing into a young child ensure that you modify the force of the breaths. If delivered too forcefully, the air will be directed into the stomach, which may cause the child to vomit, obstructing the airway.

The method used for infants is 'frog breathing' or 'puffing', where the rescuer fills his or her mouth with air and 'puffs' it into the infant's mouth. There will be adequate pressure and volume to satisfy their lung requirements, but not enough to impact on the stomach.

Indications for rescue breaths

❐ Unresponsive
❐ No *normal* breathing, although there may be brief irregular, 'gasping' breaths

Procedure for rescue breaths

✔ place your hand on the casualty's forehead and gently tilt the head back.
✔ place your fingertips under the point of the casualty's chin and lift the chin to open the airway.
✔ allow the mouth to open while maintaining chin lift
✔ take a normal breath to fill your lungs with oxygen, and place your lips around the casualty's mouth, making sure that you have a good seal
✔ blow steadily into the casualty's mouth while watching for the chest to rise
  ☛ take about one second to make the chest rise
✔ maintaining head tilt and chin lift, take your mouth away from the casualty and watch for the chest to fall
✔ repeat the sequence as above, giving two effective breaths in total
✔ stop to recheck the casualty only if they start breathing normally, otherwise do not interrupt resuscitation

Unsuccessful rescue breaths

If rescue breaths do not make the chest rise with each attempt, give 30 compressions and then before your next attempt at rescue breaths:

✔ check the casualty's mouth and remove any visible obstructions
✔ ensure that there is adequate head tilt and chin lift
△ **DO NOT** attempt more than two rescue breaths each time before returning to chest compressions

CARDIOPULMONARY RESUSCITATION (CPR)

Cardiopulmonary Resuscitation (CPR) is Rescue Breaths used in conjunction with Chest Compressions. CPR is the most effective form of active resuscitation available today and is used universally by first aiders and medical personnel alike. The technique is vital in supplying oxygen and blood circulation to the casualty and is used to 'buy time' in resuscitation of casualties in cardiac arrest.

Rescue breaths provide oxygen to the casualty's lungs and blood while chest compressions, when applied correctly pumps the oxygenated blood around the body. Effective CPR will "buy time" for a casualty by circulating blood and oxygen around the body reducing damage to vital organs such as the brain.

Indications for CPR

❑ Unresponsive

❑ No *normal* breathing, although there may be brief irregular, 'gasping' breaths

Procedure for CPR

To provide effective compressions the first aider's must compress in the centre of the casualty's chest.

✔ ensure the safety of all those at the scene

✔ check the casualty's response

✔ check the casualty's condition and send or go for help, or call 999 for an ambulance

☞ if you are on your own, leave the casualty and go for help

✔ open airway

✔ check breathing

✔ if unresponsive and not breathing

ADULTS AND CHILDREN

✔ kneel by the side of the casualty

✔ place the heel of one hand in the centre of the casualty's chest

✔ place the heel of the other hand on top of the first hand and interlock the fingers of the hands

△ **DO NOT** apply any pressure over the casualty's ribs, upper abdomen or the bottom end of the bony sternum (breastbone)

✔ position yourself directly above the casualty's chest and, with your arms straight, press down on the sternum:

☞ Adult - 4 - 5 cm

☞ Child - $1/3$ depth of chest

✔ release all the pressure on the chest without losing contact between the hands and the sternum

✔ repeat at a rate of about 100 times a minute (a little less than 2 compressions a second).

✔ compression and release should take an equal amount of time

INFANTS

✔ kneel by the side of the casualty

✔ place two fingers in the centre of the casualty's chest

✔ ensure that pressure is not applied over the casualty's ribs.

△ **DO NOT** apply any pressure over the upper abdomen or the bottom end of the bony sternum (breastbone)

✔ position yourself directly above the casualty's chest and, with your arm straight, press down on the sternum $1/3$ the depth of the chest

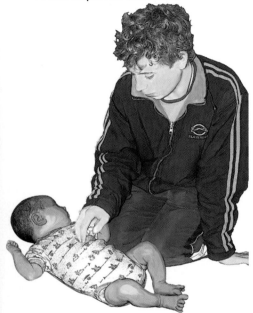

✔ release all the pressure on the chest without losing contact between the fingers and the sternum

✔ repeat at a rate of about 100 times a minute (a little less than 2 compressions a second).

✔ compression and release should take an equal amount of time

Rescue breaths - All ages

✔ place your hand on the casualty's forehead and gently tilt the head back

✔ place your fingertips under the point of the casualty's chin and lift the chin to open the airway

✔ allow the mouth to open while maintaining chin lift

✔ take a normal breath to fill your lungs with oxygen, and place your lips around the casualty's mouth, making sure that you have a good seal

✔ blow steadily into the casualty's mouth while watching for the chest to rise

☞ take about one second to make the chest rise

✔ maintaining head tilt and chin lift, take your mouth away from the casualty and watch for the chest to fall

✔ repeat the sequence as above, giving two effective breaths in total

✔ return your hands or fingers quickly to the centre of the chest and then give the next 30 compressions

✔ repeat 2 breaths

✔ repeat sequence

✔ use AED if available

Unsuccessful rescue breaths

If rescue breaths do not make the chest rise with each attempt, then before your next attempt:

✔ check the casualty's mouth and remove any visible obstructions

✔ ensure that there is adequate head tilt and chin lift

✔ **DO NOT** attempt more than two rescue breaths each time before returning to chest compressions

Chest compression only CPR

If for any reason rescue breaths can not be given, chest compressions should still be administered as some oxygen will still be circulated. Compress in the centre of the casualty's chest continuously 100 times per minute.

Re-checking for circulation

You should only stop to re-check the casualty if they start breathing normally again, otherwise do not interrupt resuscitation.

Multiple rescuers

If there is more than one rescuer present, change over the roll of performing CPR approximately every 2 minutes to reduce fatigue. Change over with minimal delay of compressions.

Defibrillation

Defibrillation is the emergency procedure where first aiders apply an electronic device called an Automated External Defibrillator (AED) to the chest of a cardiac arrest casualty and the device delivers a controlled electric shock to the casualty's heart.

When to stop CPR

❑ Qualified help arrives and takes over
❑ The casualty starts breathing normally
❑ You become physically unable to continue

When to get help

❑ If more than one rescuer is available, one should start resuscitation while another rescuer goes for assistance
❑ In children or infants if only one rescuer is available, then perform 1 minute of CPR before leaving to go for assistance
❑ If the casualty is an infant or small child it may be possible to take them with you
❑ If the collapse was sudden, not caused by trauma or poisoning and the casualty is a child with a history of heart disease, go for help immediately

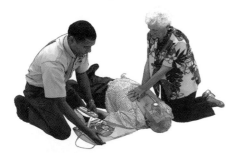

If an AED is available:

✔ turn the AED on
✔ follow the prompts
✔ press shock button if advised
✔ follow local protocols if available

AUTOMATED EXTERNAL DEFIBRILLATION

The heart is a muscular pump, approximately the same size as its owner's fist, and is located behind and slightly to the left of the breastbone. Its function is to pump oxygen-rich blood from the lungs to various parts of the body, and to pump the de-oxygenated blood from the tissues back to the lungs to take on more oxygen. Pumping blood through the lungs removes carbon dioxide and re-supplies the blood with oxygen. The newly oxygenated blood is then pumped around the body to provide oxygen and nutrients and remove waste products.

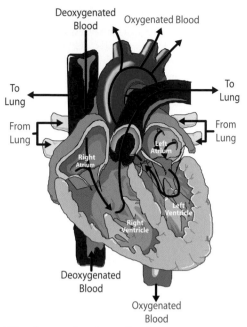

Deoxygenated Blood · Oxygenated Blood
To Lung · To Lung
From Lung · From Lung
Right Atrium · Left Atrium
Right Ventricle · Left Ventricle
Deoxygenated Blood
Oxygenated Blood

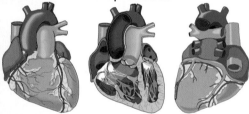

The heart's mechanical action

The heart has four chambers with one-way flaps called valves between the upper and lower chambers. The atria are the upper chambers and they receive blood that is being returned to the heart.

When the atria pump (contract), they push the blood through valves into the relaxed ventricles (lower chambers). When the ventricles contract, the right ventricle pumps blood into the lungs. It is the pressure of the blood reflected on the walls of the arteries which is felt as a pulse.

A normal healthy adult heart beats rhythmically at a rate of about 60 to 100 beats a minute when at rest. During strenuous exercise, the heart can increase the amount of blood it pumps up to four times the amount it pumps at rest within only a matter of seconds.

The heart's electrical system

The heart's electrical system causes the heart to beat, controls the heart rate (the number of beats per minute).

Given an electrical signal, the upper heart chambers (atria), contract (pump) and then relax and then passes down the separating tissue to the ventricles, causing them to contract and pump blood to the body. After the ventricles complete contracting, the electrical impulses cease, and the heart muscle relaxes.

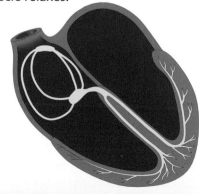

Sudden Cardiac Arrest (SCA)

Sudden cardiac arrest is the unexpected collapse of a casualty whose heart has ceased to function due to an electrical malfunction of the heart, disrupting that muscle's normal rhythm. SCA is not a heart attack, which is a problem with the plumbing of the heart. In a heart attack one or more of the arteries delivering blood to the heart is blocked, so oxygen in the blood cannot reach the heart muscle and the heart muscle is damaged.

During sudden cardiac arrest, the electrical signals to the pump suddenly become erratic. The ventricles may flutter or quiver (ventricular fibrillation), and so blood is not delivered to the body. Blood flow to the brain is reduced and the casualty loses consciousness. Death will follow unless emergency treatment is begun.

Cardiac arrest is closely linked with sudden chest pain. During SCA the heart twitches irregularly, most often in adults due to ventricular fibrillation (VF), and cannot pump oxygenated blood efficiently to the brain, lungs, and other organs. The casualty quickly stops breathing and loses consciousness.

There are no prior symptoms of sudden cardiac arrest. However, risk factors have been identified as increasing the potential for sudden cardiac arrest. Risk factors include:

❐ Family history of sudden cardiac arrest
❐ Heart failure (heart pumps poorly)
❐ History of heart rhythm disorders
❐ Previous heart attack
❐ Previous sudden cardiac arrest episode

Successful resuscitation of such a casualty depends on quick decisive action taken in sequence, like the links in a chain.

Defibrillation pads

Defibrillation pads are soft, thin foam about the size of a hand. The pads are adhesive and have a layer of gel which helps pick up the electrical signals. They normally have a cable attached to each pad. Normally a set is packaged in a special sealed pouch. As they can 'dry out', they have an expiry date printed on the package.

Pads must adhere firmly to the chest, so it is important to press the pads on firmly, including the edges of the pads.

Pads may not stick securely for several reasons. These include moisture and excessive hair on the chest. Moisture can be wiped away with a towel or cloth. You may need to clip or shave excessive hair off the chest around the pad area.

Each AED manufacture will have the instructions for applying the pads on the pad packaging and on the pads themselves. Follow these instructions as they will apply directly to the AED that is being used.

Procedure for administering an AED

✔ send someone for the AED if not already done
✔ ensure safety
  ☛ If two rescuers are present, assign tasks for each rescuer
✔ turn on the AED
✔ attach the electrode pads
  ☛ if multiple rescuers, continue CPR while the pads are attached
✔ follow the voice/visual prompts of the AED

✔ ensure that nobody touches the casualty while the AED is analysing the rhythm

If a shock is indicated:

✔ ensure that nobody touches the casualty

✔ say '**Stand Clear**'

✔ check nobody touching casualty

✔ push the shock button as directed

☛ fully-automatic AEDs will deliver the shock automatically

✔ continue to follow the voice/visual prompts of the AED

If no shock is indicated:

✔ immediately resume CPR using a ratio of 30 compressions to 2 rescue breaths.

✔ continue to follow the voice/visual prompts of the AED

Safety

An AED, just like any electrical appliance, has safety precautions to prevent injury. The AED operator is responsible for keeping all persons from touching the casualty when a shock is delivered.

❏ State a 'Clear' message. For example, say loudly "don't touch the casualty" or "Stand Clear"

❏ Look to ensure that no one is touching the casualty before pressing the shock button

BEWARE OF IMPLANTS

If a casualty has an electronic pacemaker or cardioverter implanted under the skin, ensure that the AED chest pad is positioned at least 10cm away from the pacemaker.

Ensure that the pads are not placed over a Glyceryl Trinitrate patch (GTN).

BEWARE OF GASEOUS OR OXYGEN-RICH ENVIRONMENTS

Defibrillators can cause sparks. If using oxygen to supplement resuscitation, ensure that there is no concentration of oxygen around the casualty's chest. Ensure that there is no build up of other gases around the scene.

BEWARE OF WATER

Do not use an AED if the casualty or the surroundings are saturated with water. Water is an effective transmitter of electricity and the shock may be transmitted to the AED operator.

SEPARATE THE ELECTRODES

Don't put or place the electrodes or connected pads together, or allow them to touch if the AED is 'on'. This may complete a circuit and cause an electrocution.

The AED should never be connected to anyone other than a casualty in cardiac arrest, nor should an AED be attached to a person for training or demonstration purposes.

A sign should be used to indicate the location of the AED.

3 TRAUMA

- ✍ Bleeding and shock
- ✍ Crush Injury
- ✍ Burns and scalds
- ✍ Electric shock
- ✍ Facial injuries
- ✍ Head injuries
- ✍ Spinal injuries
- ✍ Chest injuries
- ✍ Abdominal injuries
- ✍ Fractures
- ✍ Soft tissue injuries

Traumatic injury can extend from a cut finger through to major injuries involving multiple organs and body cavities. Whatever the extent of the injury first aid care follows the emergency action plan supplemented with the procedures you will find in this chapter.

By the end of this section you should be able to:

- ✚ Recognise the signs and symptoms of internal bleeding.
- ✚ Recognise the signs and symptoms of external bleeding.
- ✚ Recognise the signs and symptoms of shock.
- ✚ Manage bleeding and shock.
- ✚ Manage crush injuries.
- ✚ Recognise and manage Crush Injury Syndrome.
- ✚ Recognise the three types of burns.
- ✚ Manage burns and scalds.
- ✚ Manage facial, head, chest and abdominal injuries.
- ✚ Manage fractures.
- ✚ Apply slings for shoulder and arm injuries.

BLEEDING

The body must have enough circulating blood volume to keep the body functioning, and keep the organs supplied with oxygen. Blood consists of red cells, which convey oxygen throughout the body; white cells, which fight introduced infection; platelets, which assist in the clotting process; and plasma, the fluid portion of blood. There are between five and seven litres of blood in the average adult body which makes up 7-8% of the body weight.

Blood is moved around the body under pressure by the heart and blood vessels. Without an adequate blood volume and pressure, the human body soon collapses. Bleeding, or *haemorrhage*, poses a threat by causing both the volume and the pressure of the blood within the body to decrease through blood loss when blood vessels rupture due to a severe injury.

Bleeding is one of the common causes of death in accidents. The aim of the first aider is to reduce the loss of blood from the casualty.

External bleeding

External bleeding is usually associated with wounds. Serious wounds involve damage to blood vessels. Damage to an artery is characterised by **bright red** blood which can *spurt* with each heartbeat. Damage to veins appears as a **darker red** and tends to *flow*. Capillary damage is associated with wounds close to the skin and is a **bright red** and *oozes*.

A wound is caused when our body tissue is *torn* or *cut*. Types of wounds include *abrasions, amputations, incisions, lacerations* and *punctures.*

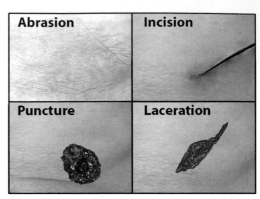

Abrasion | Incision
Puncture | Laceration

Abrasion: is a wound where the skin layers have been scraped off from a fall on a rough surface, pieces of shells, claws of animals, machinery etc. These wounds have torn or irregular edges and they tend to bleed less.

Amputation: is the severing or partial severing of part of the body, such as a limb or part of a limb.

Incision: is a wound characterised by 'slicing' as with a sharp knife or sharp piece of metal. It is often characterised by a narrow wound which has cut cleanly and bleeds extensively.

Laceration: is a jagged-edge wound with associated tissue loss, such as from a barbed wire fence injury, or where a rider's ankles, knees, elbows or wrists have abraded at speed, colliding with a road surface.

Puncture wounds are perforations, from anything from a corkscrew to a bullet, and generally with a limited external area but potentially quite deep, affecting internal organs.

Some bleeding, such as Varicose veins, can often rupture with little or no injury.

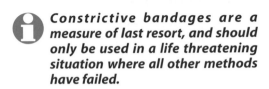

✚ CARE AND TREATMENT

Life threatening bleeding

- ☽ call **'999'** for an ambulance
- ✔ put on disposable gloves if available
- ✔ remove or cut clothing to expose the wound
- ✔ check the wound for visible foreign bodies
- ✔ apply direct pressure over the wound with a sterile or clean pad
  - ☛ the casualty may be able to apply direct pressure themselves
- ✔ lie the casualty down if not already in this position
- ✔ raise and support the injured part above the level of the heart if possible
- ✔ apply a dressing and a firm bandage to hold the pad in place
  - ☛ check circulation
  - ☛ reassess circulation every 30 minutes
- ✔ treat for shock if required
- ✔ check circulation regularly to ensure bandage is not too tight
- ✔ regularly monitor and record level of consciousness, pulse and breathing

If unable to stop the bleeding consider a constrictive bandage

- ✔ cut or remove all clothing from the upper part of the affected limb
- ✔ select a firm wide bandage (minimum 5cm) that is not too elastic
- ✔ apply bandage firmly to limb and tighten until bleeding stops
- △ **DO NOT** cover the bandage – ensure that the constrictive bandage remains easily seen

---

ⓘ *Constrictive bandages are a measure of last resort, and should only be used in a life threatening situation where all other methods have failed.*

Bleeding From Wounds

- ✔ put on disposable gloves if available
- ✔ check the wound for foreign matter
- ✔ immediately apply pressure to stop any bleeding
- ✔ bring the sides of the wound together and press firmly
- ✔ if a penetrating object is present
  - ☛ build up padding around the object for bleeding control and support
  - ☛ apply a firm roller or triangular bandage to support padding
- ✔ apply a non-stick dressing and a firm roller bandage
- ✔ immobilise and elevate the injured limb if injuries permit
- △ **DO NOT** remove any penetrating object
- △ **DO NOT** put pressure over penetrating object

Nosebleed

- ✔ put on disposable gloves if available
- ✔ have the casualty pinch the fleshy part of the nose just below the bone

✔ have the casualty lean slightly forward

✔ ask the casualty to breathe through their mouth

✔ maintain the pressure and posture for at least 10 minutes

   ☛ a longer time may be needed in hot weather or after exercise or if the casualty has high blood pressure

✔ apply cool compress to the nose, neck and forehead

✔ if bleeding persists, obtain medical aid

△ advise the casualty not to blow or pick their nose for several hours or to swallow blood

AMPUTATION

✔ treat as for *bleeding from wounds*

✔ after bleeding is controlled

   ☛ collect amputated part – keep dry, **DO NOT** wash or clean

   ☛ seal the amputated part in a plastic bag or wrap in waterproof material

   ☛ place in iced water – **DO NOT** allow the amputated part to come in direct contact with ice. *Freezing will kill tissue*

✔ ensure the amputated part goes to the hospital with the casualty. Often the part can be re-attached using microsurgery

If bleeding occurs through the existing dressing, place a second dressing over the first leaving the existing dressing in place. Remove and replace only the bandage and padding. Maintain direct pressure over the bleeding area as much as possible. Avoid disturbing the bandage or pad once the bleeding has been controlled.

Wounds can be cleaned with clean water or sodium chloride..

Internal bleeding

Internal bleeding is classified as either *visible*, in that the bleeding can be seen, or *concealed*, where no direct evidence of bleeding is obvious.

Always consider internal bleeding after injury, understanding it cannot be controlled by the first aider.

In most instances, obtaining an adequate history of the incident or illness will give the first aid provider the necessary clue as to whether internal bleeding may be present. Remember that current signs and symptoms, or the lack of them, do not necessarily indicate the casualty's condition.

Certain critical signs and symptoms may not appear until well after the incident due to the stealth of the bleed, and may only be detected by the fact that the casualty's observations worsen despite there being no visible cause.

VISIBLE INTERNAL BLEEDING

Visible internal bleeding is referred to this way because the results can be seen in bleeding from:

❏ **Anus or vagina** – usually red blood mixed with mucus

❏ **Ears** – bright, sticky blood or blood mixed with clear fluid

❏ **Lungs** – frothy, bright red blood coughed up by the casualty

❏ **Stomach, bowel or intestines** – bright, dark or tarry blood

❏ **Under the skin (bruising)** – the tissues look dark due to the blood under the skin

❏ **Urinary tract** – dark or red coloured urine

CONCEALED INTERNAL BLEEDING

Detecting internal bleeding relies upon good observations and an appreciation of the physical forces that have affected the casualty. In these cases, the first aid provider relies heavily on history, signs and symptoms. If you are unsure, assume the worst and treat for internal bleeding.

Remember to look at the important observations that may indicate internal bleeding, which include:

- ❑ Skin appearance
- ❑ Conscious state
- ❑ Pulse
- ❑ Respiration

 SIGNS AND SYMPTOMS

- ◯ pale, cool, clammy skin
- ◯ thirst
- ◯ rapid, weak pulse
- ◯ rapid, shallow breathing
- ◯ 'guarding' of the abdomen, with foetal position if lying down
- ◯ pain or discomfort
- ◯ nausea and/or vomiting
- ◯ visible swelling of the abdomen
- ◯ gradually lapsing into shock

✚ CARE AND TREATMENT

- ☏ call **'999'** for an ambulance
- ✔ put on disposable gloves if available
- ✔ if conscious – lie the casualty down with legs elevated and bent at the knees
- ✔ if unconscious – recovery position and elevate the legs if possible
- ✔ reassurance
- ✔ treat any injuries
- ✔ give nothing by mouth

CRUSH INJURY

A crush injury occurs when a body part is subjected to a high degree of pressure after being squeezed between two heavy or immobile objects.

Damage caused by a crush injury can include: laceration, fracture, bleeding, bruising and/or crush injury syndrome.

 SIGNS AND SYMPTOMS

- ◯ pain at the site
- ◯ tenderness
- ◯ associated wound and blood loss
- ◯ deformity

✚ CARE AND TREATMENT

- ☏ call **'999'** for an ambulance if required
- ✔ reassure casualty
- ✔ treat any wounds
- ✔ treat any fractures

Crush Injury Syndrome

A compressing force which traps a casualty can cause *crush injury syndrome*. This force, if applied to a large muscle mass, eg the thigh, causes the body to produce large quantities of acid and complex electrolytes, especially potassium, around the affected muscles. On release of the compressing force, the liberated blood takes the concentrated chemicals to the heart, with often fatal results. In addition, there is often a sudden loss of blood on releasing the compressing force.

Crush injury syndrome does not occur every time a casualty is trapped, but the first aid provider should consider the risk.

As a general rule, the requirement for consideration is based on three criteria:

1. A large muscle mass is involved
2. Prolonged compression
3. Compromised blood circulation

For instance, entrapment of a hand is unlikely to initiate the syndrome (no major muscle mass).

The major problem that faces the first aid provider when dealing with suspected crush injury is dissuading helpful bystanders from attempting to remove the compressing force without assessing the situation first.

 SIGNS AND SYMPTOMS

- ○ compression more than 15 minutes
- ○ large muscle mass involved
- ○ absent pulse and capillary return in the distal limb
- ○ pale, cool, clammy skin
- ○ weak, rapid pulse
- ○ usually absence of pain in the affected region
- ○ onset of shock

➕ **CARE AND TREATMENT**

- ☎ call **'999'** for an ambulance
- ✔ if compressed for less than 15 minutes
  - ✔ relieve the crushing force as quickly and gently as possible, provided it is safe to do so
- ✔ if compressed for more than 15 minutes
  - △ **DO NOT** relieve the crushing force
- ✔ reassure casualty
- ✔ treat for shock
- ✔ treat any other injuries
- ✔ be prepared to assist the medical support team

SHOCK

Shock is a life-threatening condition and should be treated as top priority, second only to attending to safety, an obstructed airway, absence of breathing, cardiac arrest or severe life threatening bleeding.

Shock is a deteriorating condition that does not allow a casualty to recover without active medical intervention.

Causes of shock

Loss of blood – this is the most common cause of shock. Blood loss may occur immediately or may be delayed. The blood loss could be either seen externally or internally within a particular system or organ.

The greater the loss of blood, the greater the chance of developing shock. A slow, steady loss of blood can also produce shock.

Abdominal emergencies – Burst appendix, perforated intestine or stomach, intestinal obstruction, pancreatitis.

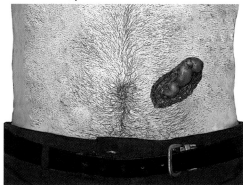

Loss of body fluids – May be due to extensive burns, dehydration, severe vomiting or diarrhoea.

Heart attack – Failure of the heart to function due to an obstructed blood supply to the heart itself can produce shock.

Sepsis or toxicity – Discharge of toxins produced by bacteria in the blood stream can produce shock.

Spinal injury – Due to the injury and the reaction of the nervous system.

Crush injuries – Injuries following explosions, building collapses etc.

As a first aider attending a casualty, you should ask yourself the following:

- ☐ *Does the injury appear* **serious?**
- ☐ *If I don't do anything to help, is the casualty likely to become* **worse?**
- ☐ *If the casualty's condition worsens,* **is death a possibility?**

If the answer to any of these questions is **'YES!'**, then you should **treat for shock**.

Observation	Healthy	Shocked
Skin Condition	Pink, warm, dry	Pale, cold, wet
Conscious State	Alert and aware of time and place	Altered, confused, aggressive
Pulse	*Per Minute*	Rapid – above upper limits
Adult	60 – 100	
Child	90 – 130	
Infant	120 – 160	
Respiration	*Per Minute*	Rapid – above upper limits
Adult	12 – 20	
Child	16 – 25	
Infant	20 – 30	

 SIGNS AND SYMPTOMS

- ○ pale, cool, clammy skin
- ○ thirst
- ○ rapid, shallow breathing
- ○ rapid, weak pulse
- ○ nausea and/or vomiting
- ○ evidence of loss of body fluids, or high temperature if sepsis present
- ○ collapse and unconsciousness
- ○ progressive 'shutdown' of body's vital functions

✚ CARE AND TREATMENT

- ☽ call **'999'** for an ambulance
- ✔ put on disposable gloves if available
- ✔ control any bleeding
- ✔ if conscious, lie the casualty down with legs elevated and bent at the knees
- ✔ if unconscious, recovery position with support under the legs to elevate them
- ✔ reassurance
- ✔ maintain body temperature, but **DO NOT** overheat
- ✔ treat any other injuries

BURNS AND SCALDS

Burns are injuries that damage and kill skin cells, and are most commonly caused by exposure to flames, hot objects, hot liquids, chemicals, radiation or a combination of these. Scalds are caused by contact with wet heat such as boiling fluids or steam. Electrical burns are less common, but have the potential to be more serious as the depth of the burn is usually greater than is apparent, and heart irregularities may occur.

As with most potentially serious injuries, prevention is better than cure. All homes should be fitted with smoke detectors. Keep hot objects, such as kettles, safely out of reach of children and make sure to turn off heaters and stoves when not in use.

Also keep all electrical wires away from water, place socket caps over all unused electrical sockets and have your leads tested and tagged regularly. Keep household chemicals out of reach of children, ensure these are well marked and their caps are screwed on tight.

Burns are most commonly caused by exposure to flames, hot objects, hot liquids, chemicals or radiation.

Scalds are caused by contact with wet heat such as boiling fluids or steam.

A doctor should see infants or children who receive any burns.

It is important that any casualty who has inhaled smoke, fumes or superheated air, or has been burnt on the face, seeks medical aid as soon as possible after the incident.

Electrical burns have the potential to be more serious as the depth of the burn is usually greater than is apparent and cardiac (heart) irregularities may occur.

Burns are classified as either:

Superficial
- ❏ Reddening (like sunburn)
- ❏ Damage to outer layer of skin only

Partial thickness
- ❏ Blistering
- ❏ Damage to outer layer of skin

Full thickness
- ❏ White or blackened areas
- ❏ Damage to all layers of skin, plus underlying structures and tissues

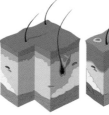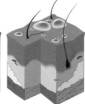

| *Superficial Thickness* | *Partial Thickness* | *Full Thickness* |

SIGNS AND SYMPTOMS

○ red, blistered, white or blackened skin
○ pain in superficial and partial thickness burns
○ signs of shock
○ breathing difficulties
○ hoarse voice and/or snoring sound when breathing

➕ CARE AND TREATMENT

✔ ensure safety
☎ call **'999'** for an ambulance
✔ put on disposable gloves if available
✔ cool only with clean water if possible and resist using other substances
  ☛ for at least 10 minutes for thermal or radiation burns
  ☛ for at least 20 minutes for chemical burns
  ☛ for at least 30 minutes for bitumen burns
    ☞ if medical assistance is delayed and the limb is completely encircled, split the bitumen lengthwise as it cools
  ☛ keep phosphorous burns wet at all times
✔ remove phosphorus particles using forceps only
✔ cover with a clean, non-stick sterile dressing (or plastic wrap etc.)
✔ remove tight clothing and objects, eg rings, jewellery
✔ treat for shock if the burn is severe
✔ ensure that contaminated or smouldering clothing is removed unless it is sticking to the skin
✔ flush chemicals from the skin, pay special attention to eyes
△ **DO NOT** break blisters

△ **DO NOT** attempt to remove bitumen from the skin or eyes
△ avoid the use of lotions and creams
△ ensure cooling is not excessive resulting in shivering

Burns to the face may have an effect on the casualty's breathing, and these effects may take some time to appear.

Seek medical aid if the:

❒ Burn is larger than the casualty's palm
❒ Casualty has inhaled smoke, fumes or superheated air
❒ Casualty is an infant or child
❒ Burns involve the hands, face or genitals
❒ Burn was caused by:
  ⊃ lasers
  ⊃ industrial microwave equipment
  ⊃ infra-red or ultra-violet rays
  ⊃ nuclear radiation

ELECTRIC SHOCK

⚠ **WARNING**: casualty may be LIVE!

Be careful not to touch the casualty's skin before the electrical source is disconnected. Be alert for the presence of water or conducting materials which may be in contact with the casualty.

The human body is an efficient conductor of electricity. When a casualty receives an electric shock from a household appliance or a power line, the electricity is conducted through the body. A casualty may receive significant burns or the electric shock may interfere with the heart's electrical system. Burns to the casualty may be internal and greater than they appear on the surface.

Domestic voltage

It is urgent that the casualty be disconnected from the electrical source, either by:

- ❒ Turning off the power supply and disconnecting any plugs from the outlet and isolating the electricity supply at the main power board if possible; or
- ❒ Removing the casualty from the electrical source by pushing or pulling them with non conducting materials, eg, wooden stick/board, rope, curtains or blanket.

Be careful not to touch the casualty's skin before the electrical source is disconnected, and be alert for the presence of water or conducting materials with which they may be in contact.

High voltage

High voltage electrocution involves an extreme degree of risk to rescuers. If the electrical source is part of the electrical distribution grid (poles, pylons, underground cables, transformers or stations) you must not enter the area until electrical authorities have certified it safe.

You can do nothing for a casualty within the zone of danger! Protect yourself and others.

SIGNS AND SYMPTOMS
- ○ difficult, or absent breathing
- ○ absent, weak or irregular pulse
- ○ evidence of burns
- ○ evidence of fractures
- ○ entrance and exit wound burns
- ○ collapse and unconsciousness

 ## CARE AND TREATMENT
- ☾ call *'999'* for an ambulance
- ✔ inform electrical authorities if high voltage involved
- ✔ put on disposable gloves if available
- ✔ if in respiratory arrest – commence rescue breaths
- ✔ if in cardiac arrest – commence CPR
- ✔ cool and cover burns with non-stick dressings
- ✔ reassurance

FACIAL INJURIES

Facial injuries require special attention because they can damage several of the 'senses', the airway and possibly result in permanent disfigurement. Contusions, lacerations and puncture wounds can permanently disfigure the casualty. In the case of the cheek and chin, injuries also may result in loss of function if facial nerves or muscles are injured.

Ear injuries

The ear has two functions; as the receptacle of the auditory senses (hearing), and as the organ of balance. Injuries to the ear usually affect hearing function rather than balance.

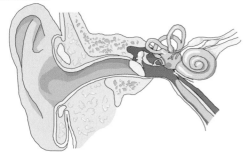

Children are especially at risk of ear damage by inserting small objects into the ear canal. This can have serious effects on the tympanic membrane or 'eardrum'. An old, but sensible, saying is that 'nothing smaller than the elbow should be poked in the ear'.

The eardrum is easily damaged. Holes or tears may be caused by swimming and diving beneath the surface, change in altitude (flying), or by vigorous nose-blowing when 'stuffed up' with a cold or flu. Minor eardrum injuries usually spontaneously repair themselves over a period of hours.

✚ CARE AND TREATMENT

EAR OBSTRUCTION
- ✔ if an insect, attempt to float it out with warm water or clean light vegetable oil
- ✔ if immovable object, seek medical aid
- △ **DO NOT** poke anything into the ear

RUPTURED EARDRUM
- ✔ place cover over affected ear to guard against infection
- ✔ seek medical aid
- △ avoid using eardrops unless directed by a doctor
- △ avoid swimming or water sports

Eye injuries

The eye is a robust but delicate organ. It can sustain quite severe damage and, with the proper treatment, recover to its former state. In some instances, however, a seemingly 'minor' injury can be permanently disabling.

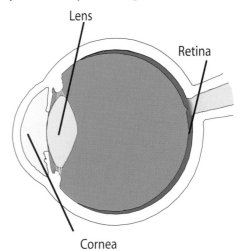

Lens

Retina

Cornea

Always consider preventing eye injuries and taking sufficient protective measures (such as protective glasses or goggles).

Generally, eye injuries are considered as either minor or major injuries.

MINOR EYE INJURIES

These are injuries where the eye has come in contact with a foreign object causing minor irritation, or the object remains on the surface of the eye. It is characterised by a bloodshot eye, irritation and an urge to rub the eye.

✚ CARE AND TREATMENT

✔ irrigate the eye and wash the object out

✔ if this fails, touch the corner of a clean wet cloth to the object and lift it off the surface

✔ refer to medical aid if vision is affected

✔ cover the affected eye if appropriate

△ avoid 'pushing' the object around the eye's surface

△ only use eye-drops if prescribed by a doctor

MAJOR EYE INJURIES

These are injuries that involve the penetration of the body of the eye, or involve severe blunt trauma to the eye.

These injuries are characterised by blood in the eye, penetrating objects, disturbance of vision, protrusion of eye contents, and severe pain and spasms. Casualty care in this case is critical, and should be left to the experts.

✚ CARE AND TREATMENT

✔ lay the casualty flat with complete rest

☾ call **'999'** for an ambulance

✔ cover the affected eye

✔ if tolerated by the casualty, cover the unaffected eye, but remove it if the casualty becomes anxious

✔ reassurance

△ avoid attempting to remove any penetrating object

△ attempts to transport the casualty other than by ambulance should be resisted

△ **DO NOT** use eye-drops

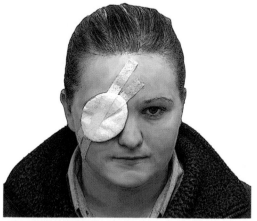

WELDER'S FLASH

Flash burn and welder's flash is the result of staring or inadvertently looking at the intense light caused during metal welding, while not wearing the correct eye protection.

Care must be taken to supervise children if welding is being conducted near them, and they should be removed from the location. The damage caused to the eye's cornea by exposure to this intense light can be painful and, in some cases, permanent.

CARE AND TREATMENT

✔ apply cool compresses and cover the eyes with pads

✔ urgent medical attention if pain or spots persist

Tooth injuries

The structure of the tooth includes dentin, pulp and other tissues, blood vessels and nerves embedded in the bony jaw. Above the gum line, the tooth is protected by the hard enamel covering.

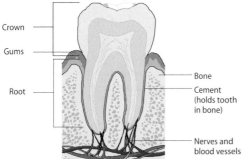

Crown

Gums

Root

Bone

Cement (holds tooth in bone)

Nerves and blood vessels

When a tooth is knocked out, appropriate emergency medical and dental care is necessary. If a child is 7 or more it is likely to be a second or permanent tooth. A second or permanent tooth can often be saved if prompt action is taken, and the tooth is handled carefully.

The delicate tissue covering the root must be protected to ensure successful re-implantation.

If a child is 6 or less it is likely to be a baby or primary tooth. Baby teeth may become injured after a fall and turn grey in colour. Treatment is not always necessary, but it is best to have the dentist examine the child as soon as possible.

CARE AND TREATMENT

When a baby or toddler injures gums or teeth:

✔ if there is bleeding, put cold water on a piece of gauze and apply pressure to the site

✔ offer the casualty an icy pole or ice cube to suck, to reduce swelling

✔ call your dentist. They will probably want to see the child to assess the need for realignment, or removal of a very loose tooth

If a permanent tooth is knocked out:

✔ hold the tooth by the crown (chewing edge), not the root

✔ rinse the tooth immediately with saline solution or milk, avoid scrubbing material off it. If this is not possible, wrap in plastic cling wrap

✔ if the casualty will co-operate, replace the tooth gently in its socket

✔ have the casualty bite down gently on a gauze pad to keep the tooth in place

✔ if the tooth cannot be re-inserted, put it in milk which is a good preservative because its chemical make-up is compatible with teeth

- ✔ if milk is not available, the tooth can be placed in the casualty's mouth between the teeth and cheek, if old enough not to swallow the tooth. If this is not possible, wrap in plastic cling wrap
- ✔ give the casualty a gauze pad or handkerchief to gently bite down on, which will help control bleeding and ease the pain
- ✔ see a dentist right away, within 20 minutes if possible
- △ **DO NOT** replace the tooth or place anything in the mouth of a drowsy or unconscious casualty

If the tooth can't be re-implanted, control bleeding by placing a gauze pad in the tooth socket, and then get the casualty to bite gently down on the pad. Avoid rinsing out the mouth because this can interfere with blood clotting.

If the gums are bleeding, put cold water on a piece of gauze and push it between the lips and gums. Have the casualty hold pressure on the bleeding site.

HEAD INJURIES

Injuries to the head are always regarded as serious because they can inflict damage to the brain and spinal cord as well as damaging the bone and soft tissue. As a result head injuries can be devastating to the casualty.

Head injuries can be invisible to the eye. In many instances, a casualty who appeared unaffected after an incident, suddenly collapses with life-threatening symptoms some hours later. This may be due to the sudden movement of the head forward and backward on impact which may cause a small bleed in the brain that eventually increases and applies excessive pressure on the brain tissue. Such injuries can easily mislead the first aid provider by not exhibiting the expected signs and symptoms immediately after an incident.

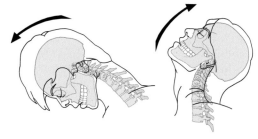

As a first aid provider you should always take head injuries seriously. Always check the patient's response and whether they have any alteration of consciousness.

Look at the history of the incident and the mechanism of injury. If in your opinion, the patient's conscious state is altered or the incident had the potential to cause serious injury, assume the worst and treat as a serious head injury.

Head injuries are generally classified as:

- ❑ **Open** – a head injury with an associated head wound
- ❑ **Closed** – with no obvious sign of injury

In some instances, serious head injury is readily identified by certain signs peculiar to the injury.

Clear fluid oozing from the nose or ears. This is cerebro-spinal fluid (CSF), which surrounds the brain. When a fracture occurs, usually at the base of the skull, the fluid leaks out under pressure into the ear and nose canals.

'Black eyes' and bruising. The kinetic energy from a blow which is transmitted through the head and brain is expelled through soft tissue, eg the eyes, and behind the ears ('Battle's sign'). Bruising at these points indicates that the head has suffered exposure to considerable force.

Remember, just because a casualty has two black eyes (Raccoon eyes), this does not necessarily mean they were struck in the face. 'Raccoon eyes' may indicate a forceful impact elsewhere on the skull.

Blurred, or double, vision is common with concussed casualties. It indicates that the brain has been dealt a blow that has temporarily affected its ability to correctly process the sight senses.

Concussion is a closed head injury. Of all the head injuries, the severity of this is often underestimated, and many casualties have succumbed several hours after the incident. Be especially observant during contact sports or activities involving children – the myth that you can 'run off' your concussion by playing on is a dangerous attitude, and has caused grief to many players, parents and coaches when the casualty eventually collapses. Concussion is potentially very serious and an indifferent attitude is to be discouraged.

Facial injuries are also head injuries, and the first aid provider should not be unduly distracted by obvious facial injuries and forget to assess the casualty for associated brain injury. Facial injuries are also a complication where the airway is concerned.

 SIGNS AND SYMPTOMS

Some, or all of the following:

- ○ head wounds
- ○ deformation of the skull
- ○ altered/deteriorating level of consciousness
- ○ evidence of CSF leaking from ears or nose
- ○ may have unequal pupils
- ○ headache

- ○ 'raccoon eyes' or 'Battle's sign'
- ○ nausea and/or vomiting
- ○ restlessness and irritability, confusion
- ○ blurred or double vision
- ○ 'snoring' respirations if unconscious

✚ CARE AND TREATMENT

- ☽ call **'999'** for an ambulance
- ✔ apply a cervical collar only if trained to do so
- ✔ treat any wounds
- ✔ complete rest
- ✔ if unconscious or drowsy, put casualty in the recovery position while supporting the cervical spine
- ✔ allow any CSF to drain freely – if in recovery position, put the injured side down with a pad over the ear to allow drainage
- △ **DO NOT** allow concussed casualties to 'play on'

SPINAL INJURIES

The spinal column consists of a series of interconnected bones, called vertebrae, which enclose the *spinal cord*, an integral part of the central nervous system. It is the spinal cord and its attached nerves which provides the means by which we breathe, move and use our senses.

Between each vertebra are discs of cartilage that act as shock absorbers and allow the spinal column a degree of flexibility. The spine is divided into five areas:

- ❒ The **cervical** spine (neck), 7 vertebrae
- ❒ The **thoracic** spine (chest), 12 vertebrae
- ❒ The **lumbar** spine (back), 5 vertebrae
- ❒ Fused vertebrae of the **sacrum**
- ❒ A small vertebra called the **coccyx**

Any injury to the spinal cord has serious ramifications for our ability to function normally, and an injury, or 'lesion', of the cord may cause quadriplegia (complete or partial paralysis of all four limbs); paraplegia (complete or partial paralysis of the lower limbs only); loss of: skin sensation, bowel, bladder and/or sexual function as well as chronic painful conditions, depending on the location of the injury along the spinal cord.

The nearer the head the lesion occurs, the more serious it is, affecting all levels of the body below it and potentially causing death if the nerves to the heart and lungs are involved. Even if the casualty is not affected to these degrees of severity, spinal injury may cause chronic back pain and restricted spinal flexibility.

Spinal injuries can be caused by a variety of physical incidents. A common cause of spinal injuries is motorcycle accidents. Riders and pillion passengers are thrown unprotected to the roadway and invariably land heavily in an awkward manner, putting stress on the spinal column. Carefully assessing the history of the incident and the mechanism of injury will benefit the first aid provider before they apply active treatment. Road traffic accidents, diving accidents and sporting accidents provide the majority of spinal casualties.

All head injured and unconscious patients potentially have spinal injuries as well

SIGNS AND SYMPTOMS

- ○ history of the trauma, especially high speed accidents or contact sports
- ○ pulse may be fast or slow and is not generally a helpful indication of presence or severity of a spinal injury
- ○ unnatural posture
- ○ may have pale, cool, clammy skin
- ○ 'tingling', unusual, or absent feeling in limbs
- ○ absence of pain in limbs despite other injuries to these areas
- ○ inability to move arms and/or legs, or weakness of movement
- ○ onset of shock
- ○ uncontrolled penile erection ("priapism") occasionally occurs

✚ CARE AND TREATMENT

- ✔ If airway is not open, use jaw thrust or manual opening of the jaw rather than extending the neck
- ✔ if unable to control airway – carefully remove the helmet while ensuring the minimum of neck movement
- ① call **'999'** for an ambulance
- ✔ extreme care in initial examination
- ✔ always maintain the casualty's head in line with the shoulders and spine using manual support. Ensure the head is supported, not pulled or pushed in any direction

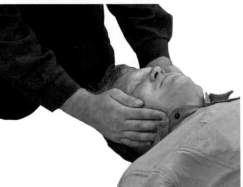

- ✔ if trained to, apply cervical collar
- ✔ position on spinal stretcher and use head-immobilisation device if trained to do so and equipment available
- ✔ treat for shock
- ✔ treat any other injuries
- ✔ maintain body heat
- ✔ if movement required, 'log roll' using 2-3 assistants

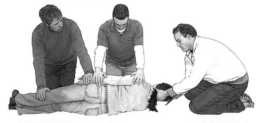

Spinal shock

Spinal shock refers to changes in blood pressure associated with injury to the spine. The blood pressure is usually lower than normal (as in shock due to blood loss), however, the pulse is usually normal or slow (the opposite of shock due to blood loss). The skin may be cold and clammy as a result.

Helmet removal

Helmets should only be removed if you intend to perform CPR or if the helmet is impeding proper airway management. Otherwise, leave helmet removal to the experts. The helmet could be helping prevent (further) spinal or head injuries.

Immobilise the casualty's head and spine by having one person place their hands on either side of the casualty's head (palms inwards) to keep it from moving. If you can, immobilise the neck and/or spine by placing rolled towels, articles of clothing, etc. on both sides of the neck and/or body, but don't interfere with the casualty's airway or breathing.

Cervical collar

A cervical collar helps immobilise the neck where cervical injury is suspected. First aiders trained in their use should apply a cervical collar, though it requires two people to apply correctly.

- ✔ the first rescuer applies manual support to the head and neck
- ✔ if the collar is adjustable, or several sizes are available, measure the correct size according to the manufacturer's instructions
- ✔ the second rescuer slides the front of the collar along the casualty's chest and positions the chin piece

- ✔ the second rescuer gently wraps the ends of the collar snugly around the casualty's neck
- ✔ the second rescuer secures the collar with the Velcro tab
- ✔ ensure collar is firm and comfortable, adjust if necessary
- ✔ maintain support to the head and neck during all adjustments

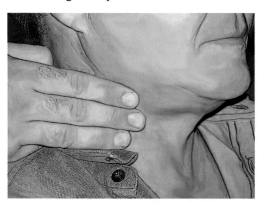

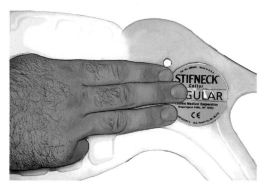

CHEST INJURIES

Chest injuries are difficult for the first aid provider to manage, and casualties with these injuries should be referred to medical aid as a matter of priority.

The major chest injuries encountered by the first aid provider are fractured ribs, flail chest and penetrating chest wounds.

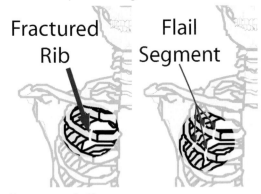

Fractured Rib

Flail Segment

Fractured ribs

Ribs are composed of successive layers of flat bone, which give the ribs their flexibility or 'spring'. When ribs fracture, often the 'spring' is reduced, rather than the entire bone being detached from the spinal column or the sternum.

Rib injuries cause distress because the casualty has difficulty breathing.

 SIGNS AND SYMPTOMS

○ history of trauma to the chest
○ pale, cool skin
○ pain at the site, especially when breathing in
○ rapid pulse
○ rapid shallow breathing
○ 'guarding' of the injury

✚ CARE AND TREATMENT

✔ bind the upper arm on the injured side to the body
✔ place the arm on the injured side in a 'collar and cuff' sling to act as a splint
✔ seek medical aid
✔ observe for breathing difficulties

Flail chest

Flail chest is an injury to the ribs where a section of the rib cage has been detached due to multiple fractures. Generally there is an associated collapsed lung (pneumothorax). Flail chest should be considered a life-threatening injury due to its complications.

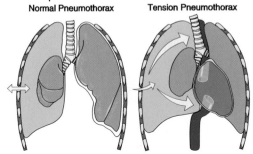

Normal Pneumothorax   Tension Pneumothorax

 SIGNS AND SYMPTOMS

○ pale, cool clammy skin
○ rapid, weak pulse
○ shallow, difficult breathing
○ paradoxical chest movements, where the injured area moves in the opposite direction to the rest of the chest
○ cyanosis (bluish skin)
○ pain, especially when breathing in

✚ CARE AND TREATMENT

- ☾ call **'999'** for an ambulance
- ✔ apply a firm pad over the flail section
- ✔ apply a firm bandage in place
- ✔ position the casualty in a posture of comfort, usually sitting
- ✔ if unconscious, position on the injured side
- ✔ reassurance
- ✔ observe carefully for signs of breathing difficulties

Penetrating chest wound

A penetrating chest wound is where the object may still be in place in the wall of the chest, or it may be an open wound left by the object, eg a stab wound, or bullet wound.

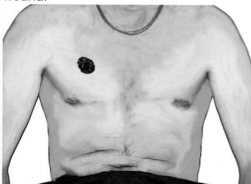

If the object is still in place **DO NOT** remove it. If it is too long or too awkward to manage (eg a tree branch), obtain urgent expert assistance and resist removing or cutting the object yourself.

SIGNS AND SYMPTOMS

- ○ history of the incident
- ○ object still in place
- ○ open wound in the chest wall (look for both entry and exit wounds)

- ○ pale, cool, clammy skin
- ○ rapid, weak pulse
- ○ rapid, shallow breathing
- ○ cyanosis (bluish skin)
- ○ may be pain at the site
- ○ onset of shock

✚ CARE AND TREATMENT

- ☾ call **'999'** for an ambulance
- ✔ if object is still in place, stabilise with a pad around entry wound
- ✔ if wound is open, apply plastic or a non-stick pad, taped on three sides only leaving bottom side un-taped to allow for air to escape from the chest. A gloved hand can be also be used to seal the wound until more suitable material is available
- ✔ posture casualty in position of comfort
- ✔ reassurance
- ✔ observe for breathing difficulties

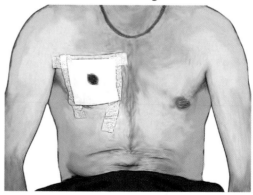

ABDOMINAL INJURIES

Abdominal injuries are caused by blunt or penetrating trauma and can involve internal bleeding or the exposure of the internal organs to air. Such injuries invariably affect vital organs. The first aid provider should be alert for shock due to internal bleeding regardless of the injury cause or whether there is a wound or not.

Blunt or penetrating trauma

Initial first aid treatment is the same whether the injury is penetrating or caused blunt trauma, eg a severe blow to the abdomen without any visible wound.

 SIGNS AND SYMPTOMS

○ history of the incident
○ pale, cool, clammy skin
○ may be evidence of wound
○ rapid, weak pulse, with evidence of shock
○ rapid, shallow breathing
○ abdominal rigidity
○ 'guarding' of abdomen – foetal position if lying down
○ may be incontinent

 CARE AND TREATMENT

☽ call **'999'** for an ambulance
✔ stop any bleeding
✔ stabilise any object where it is, and pad around the wound
✔ if the wound permits, and the casualty is conscious, lay casualty on back and elevate legs bent at the knees
✔ reassurance
△ avoid removing or touching penetrating objects

Evisceration

Evisceration is the protrusion of abdominal organs from a wound in the abdomen.

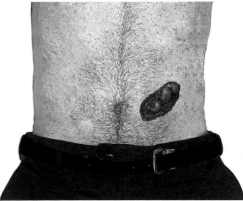

Care must be taken not to apply material to the wound that will stick to the organs. It should be noted that often there is little pain associated with this type of injury, and the casualty may walk around or offer to help.

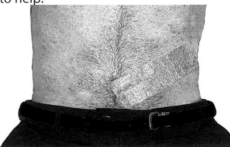

SIGNS AND SYMPTOMS

○ obvious protrusion of organs
○ pale, cool, clammy skin
○ rapid, weak pulse, with evidence of shock
○ rapid, shallow breathing
○ may be faecal odour if organs have been lacerated
○ anxiety
○ nausea

CARE AND TREATMENT

① call **'999'** for an ambulance
✔ cover organs with non-stick dressing (if unavailable, clean dressing kept wet or plastic wrap)
✔ place supporting bandage over wound
✔ place casualty flat with legs bent
✔ reassurance
✔ if unconscious, recovery position with legs bent
△ **DO NOT** attempt to replace organs

FRACTURES

There are 206 bones in the human body. The skeleton holds our skin up, and bones act as factories for producing blood and essential blood cells through bone marrow. Bones are also integral to the body's strength.

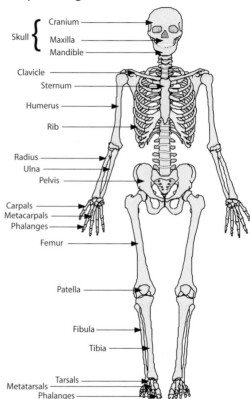

Some bones have a protective function (skull), some a supporting function (pelvis), while others are for movement (fingers).

When a bone is broken, or fractured, it affects not only blood production and function, but there can be complications associated with the muscles, tendons, nerves and blood vessels that are attached, or are close, to the bone.

Fractures are generally classified as:

- ❑ **Open** – where there is a wound exposing the fracture site, or the bone is protruding from the skin.
- ❑ **Closed** – where the bone has fractured but has no obvious external wound.

- ❑ **Complicated** – which may involve damage to associated vital organs and major blood vessels as a result of the fracture.

Immobilisation is the preferred way to manage fractured limbs as it helps reduce movement and the pain associated with fractures. Immobilise the limb with a natural splint, such as another part of the body, improvised splints, cardboard, wooden or air splints.

Fractures may be caused a number of ways:

- ❑ **Direct force**; where sufficient force is applied to cause the bone to fracture at the point of impact.
- ❑ **Indirect force**; where force or kinetic energy, applied to a large, strong bone, is transmitted up the limb, causing the weakest bones to fracture.
- ❑ **Spontaneous** or **spasm-induced**; where fractures are associated with disease and/or muscular spasms. These are usually associated with the elderly, and people with specific diseases affecting the bones.

Always exercise care when assessing an elderly casualty as the condition known as osteoporosis or 'Chalky Bones' causes bones to fracture easily, often in several places. Always suspect a fracture if an elderly person complains of pain or loss of power to a limb. Be especially aware of fractures at the neck of the femur (near the hip), a very common fracture in the elderly.

Young children are also prone to fractures. Arm and wrist fractures are common with children. As young bones do not harden for some years, children's fractures tend to 'bend and splinter', similar to a broken branch on a tree – hence the common name 'greenstick fracture'.

SIGNS AND SYMPTOMS

- ○ pale, cool, clammy skin
- ○ rapid, weak pulse
- ○ pain at the site
- ○ tenderness
- ○ loss of power to limb
- ○ associated wound and blood loss
- ○ associated organ damage
- ○ nausea
- ○ deformity

CARE AND TREATMENT

Care and treatment of fractures relies on immobilising and adequately splinting the injury. If the fracture is particularly complex, the wound associated with an open fracture maybe difficult to control.

If the pulse further down the limb cannot be restored by gentle and careful adjustment of the limb or with minor traction, the limb should be stabilised where it is.

Do not spend time attempting to splint instead of calling for urgent ambulance transport.

Circulation must be checked after a splint or sling has been applied. If the limb swells this will make the bandages tighter and this may cause circulation problems.

Indications that a bandage may be too tight include:

- ☐ Absent pulse below the bandage
- ☐ Pale/blue appearance below the bandage
- ☐ Lack of warmth below the bandage
- ☐ Pain
- ☐ Swelling
- ☐ Tingling or loss of feeling in fingers or toes

Generally, fractured limbs should be kept immobile until medical assistance arrives. However, in remote areas or where it is some time from medical aid, you may be required to treat as follows:

Fractured Arm/Collar Bone

- ✔ check for warmth or pulse to the hand, if no circulation:
  - ☛ if possible, gently and carefully adjust the position of the limb until pulse returns
- ✔ treat any wounds
- ✔ pad bony prominences
- ✔ apply adequate splint
- ✔ secure splint above and below fracture
- ✔ reassess pulse or return of colour/warmth after splint applied
- ✔ apply appropriate sling (*see page 72*)
- ✔ fractured lower arm
  - ☛ apply arm sling

- ✔ fractured upper arm
  - ☛ apply collar and cuff sling
- ✔ fractured collar bone
  - ☛ apply elevated sling
- ✔ reassess pulse or return of colour/warmth after sling applied
- ✔ adjust bandages or sling if required

Fractured Leg

- ✔ check for warmth or pulse to the foot, if no circulation:
  - ☛ if possible, gently and carefully adjust the position of the limb until pulse returns
- ✔ treat any wounds
- ✔ immobilise the limb
- ✔ pad bony prominences
- ✔ reassess circulation below injury
- ✔ adjust bandages if required

Fractured Pelvis

- ☽ call **'999'** for an ambulance
- ✔ check for pulses in both legs
- ✔ bend legs at knees, elevate lower legs slightly and support on pillows or similar
- ✔ support both hips with folded blankets either side
- ✔ discourage attempts to urinate
- ✔ adjust bandages if required

Care must be exercised with a suspected fractured pelvis. This injury may have serious complications. The casualty should always be transported by ambulance and not by alternative means unless absolutely essential.

Fractured Jaw

A common injury in certain contact sports is dislocation, or fracture, of the lower jaw (mandible). The casualty will have pain in the jaw, be unable to speak properly, and may have trouble swallowing.

- call **'999'** for an ambulance
- ✔ support the jaw
  - ☛ sit the casualty leaning slightly forward
  - ☛ rest the injured jaw on a pad held by the casualty
- △ **DO NOT** apply a bandage to support the jaw.

Observe the casualty carefully for signs of breathing difficulties and any indication they are becoming drowsy or unconscious.

Dislocations

Dislocations involve the displacement of bone from a joint. These injuries are often underestimated, and can have serious consequences in the form of damage to nerves and blood vessels. Many people have joints which dislocate easily due to a congenital condition, or weak ligaments, stretched by previous repeated dislocations.

 SIGNS AND SYMPTOMS

- ○ sudden pain in the affected joint
- ○ loss of power and movement
- ○ deformity and swelling of the joint
- ○ tenderness
- ○ may have some temporary paralysis of the injured limb

✚ CARE AND TREATMENT

- ✔ RICE *(see page 74)*
- ✔ support limb in position of comfort
- ✔ seek medical aid
- ✔ any attempt to reduce a dislocation is only to be made by a doctor

Slings

Use slings to support an injured arm, or to supplement treatment for another injury such as fractured ribs. Generally, the most effective sling is made with a triangular bandage. Every first aid kit, no matter how small, should have at least one of these bandages as essential items.

Although triangular bandages are preferable, any material, eg tie, belt, or piece of thick twine or rope, can be used in an emergency. If no likely material is at hand, an injured arm can be adequately supported by inserting it inside the casualty's shirt or blouse. Similarly, a safety pin applied to a sleeve and secured to clothing on the chest may suffice.

There are essentially three types of sling; the arm sling for injuries to the forearm, the elevated sling for injuries to the shoulder, and the 'collar-and-cuff' or clove hitch for injuries to the upper arm and as supplementary support to fractured ribs.

After applying any sling, always check the circulation to the limb by feeling for the pulse at the wrist, or squeezing a fingernail and observing for change of colour in the nail bed.

All slings must be in a position that is comfortable for the casualty. Never force an arm into the 'right position'.

ARM SLING

- ✔ Support the injured forearm approximately parallel to the ground with the wrist slightly higher than the elbow
- ✔ Place an opened triangular bandage between the body and the arm, with its apex towards the elbow
- ✔ Extend the upper point of the bandage over the shoulder on the uninjured side
- ✔ Bring the lower point up over the arm, across the shoulder on the injured side to join the upper point and tie firmly with a reef knot
- ✔ Ensure the elbow is secured by folding the excess bandage over the elbow and securing with a safety pin

- ✔ Extend the upper point of the bandage over the uninjured shoulder
- ✔ Tuck the lower part of the bandage under the injured arm, bring it under the elbow and around the back and extend the lower point up to meet the upper point at the shoulder
- ✔ Tie firmly with a reef knot
- ✔ Secure the elbow by folding the excess material and applying a safety pin, then ensure that the sling is tucked under the arm giving firm support

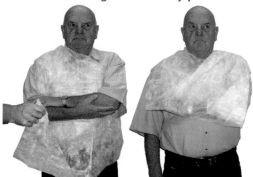

ELEVATED SLING

- ✔ Support the casualty's arm with the elbow beside the body and the hand extended towards the uninjured shoulder
- ✔ Place an opened triangular bandage over the forearm and hand, with the apex towards the elbow

'COLLAR-AND-CUFF' (CLOVE HITCH)

- ✔ allow the elbow to hang naturally at the side and place the hand extended towards the shoulder on the uninjured side
- ✔ using a narrow fold triangular bandage, form a clove hitch by forming two loops – one towards you, one away from you
- ✔ put the loops together by sliding your hands under the loops and closing with a "clapping" motion. If you are experienced at forming a clove hitch, then apply a clove hitch directly on the wrist, but take care not to move the injured arm

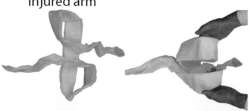

✔ slide the clove hitch over the hand and gently pull it firmly to secure the wrist

✔ extend the points of the bandage to either side of the neck and tie firmly with a reef knot

✔ allow the arm to hang comfortably. Should further support be required, eg for support to fractured ribs, apply triangular bandages around the body and upper arm to hold the arm firmly against the chest

SOFT TISSUE INJURIES

Soft tissue injuries are those injuries affecting the joints and muscles of injured, but not fractured, limbs. Sprains, strains and dislocations are considered soft tissue injuries, with some authorities also including bruising.

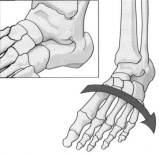

Treating soft tissue injuries is based on resting the injured part, applying ice packs to limit swelling and reduce pain, applying a firm compression bandage as support, and elevating the limb. This treatment is known as '**RICE**'.

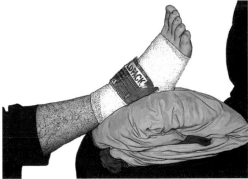

❒ **R**est – The injured part is rested immediately to reduce internal bleeding and swelling and to prevent the injury from becoming worse.

❒ **I**ce – Ice helps to limit inflammation and reduce pain by causing the blood vessels to constrict, restricting the amount of fluid and swelling in the injured part.

Chest cramps (Stiches)

Usually caused by cramps of the muscles between the ribs, or the diaphragm high in the abdomen brought on by exertion. The pain can occur during vigorous exercise, such as running.

 SIGNS AND SYMPTOMS
- ○ sharp, spasmodic pain in the chest just below the rib cage
- ○ difficulty in standing upright
- ○ gasping respirations

 CARE AND TREATMENT
- ✔ rest in a cool area
- ✔ have casualty stretch the cramping muscle
- ✔ the casualty should take deep breaths
- ✔ cool drink

Groin injuries

Caused by a blow to the groin, or by over-stretching the associated muscles. Groin pain mostly results from musculotendinous injuries.

 SIGNS AND SYMPTOMS
- ○ pain to the region of the groin
- ○ sometimes nausea or vomiting
- ○ unable to stand upright

 CARE AND TREATMENT
- ✔ place casualty on thier back with knees slightly bent
- ✔ apply ice pack
- ✔ seek medical aid

Muscle cramps

Caused by over-stretching muscles, or by involuntary muscle contraction. They may also be associated with loss of fluid due to excessive sweating or heavy exercise.

 SIGNS AND SYMPTOMS
- ○ sudden and sharp muscle pain
- ○ loss of power
- ○ stiffening or spasms of the muscles
- ○ hard, bulging muscle

 CARE AND TREATMENT
- ✔ apply ice pack
- ✔ slow gentle stretching
- △ **DO NOT** massage the affected muscles

'Winding'

Caused by a blow to the abdomen which temporarily 'paralyses' the diaphragm.

 SIGNS AND SYMPTOMS
- ○ gasping attempts to breathe
- ○ lack of chest movement
- ○ bending at the waist and 'guarding' the abdomen

CARE AND TREATMENT

✔ lay the casualty down
✔ reassurance
△ **DO NOT** pump' the casualty's legs

'Tennis elbow'

This is an injury to the muscles and tendons on the outside of the elbow that results from overuse or repetitive stress. Severe cases also involve the ligaments.

 SIGNS AND SYMPTOMS

○ the onset of pain on the outside of the elbow
○ difficulty holding, lifting, carrying or gripping objects
○ stiffness or reduced elbow and hand movement
○ difficulty extending the forearm fully

✚ **CARE AND TREATMENT**

✔ RICE
✔ support the arm in a sling

Shin splints

Shin splints is the name given to pain at the front of the lower leg and describes of a number of symptoms of which there could be a number of causes. The most common cause of pain is inflammation of the sheath surrounding the bone of the tibia.

This injury is due to a strain of the long flexor muscle of the toes. This is an injury common to runners and footballers and is an overuse injury.

 SIGNS AND SYMPTOMS

○ tenderness on the inside of the shin
○ lower leg pain.
○ swelling.
○ pain when the toes or foot are bent downwards
○ redness over the inside of the shin

✚ **CARE AND TREATMENT**

✔ rest
✔ apply a ice pack
✔ repetitive injury should be examined and treated by a medical professional

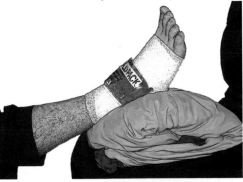

Other sports injuries should be treated as they present, and medical aid sought as a matter of course. Injuries sustained by many athletes are chronic, and recur on a regular basis. If these injuries are in the form of sprains and strains, they may require support in the form of strapping or taping.

Provided that a doctor has assessed the athlete, and that no other form of treatment has been prescribed, strapping may be applied by a qualified person to support the injured part.

4

MEDICAL EMERGENCIES

- Anaphylaxis
- Asthma
- Croup and epiglottitis
- Diabetes
- Drowning
- Epilepsy
- Fainting
- Febrile convulsions
- Heart conditions
- Hyperventilation
- Poisoning
- Stroke

This section covers common medical conditions that may threaten a casualty's life unless quick action is taken to treat those conditions. The early identification and treatment of these conditions can save a life.

By the end of this section you should be able to:

+ Recognise and manage a range of medical emergencies.
+ Recognise and manage poisoning.

ANAPHYLAXIS

Anaphylaxis is the most severe form of an allergic reaction and has the potential to be life-threatening. Anaphylaxis occurs after exposure to an allergen such as food (eg nuts), herbal remedies, latex, insect stings (eg bees), or medicine, to which a person is already extremely sensitive.

It takes only 1 to 2 minutes for a mild allergic reaction to escalate to anaphylaxis. Some casualties may find that the symptoms they experience are always mild. For example, there may be a tingling or itching in the mouth and nothing more.

Anaphylaxis is a preventable and treatable event. The most important aspect of the management of casualties with life-threatening allergic reaction is avoidance of any known triggers such as:

- ❑ **Food** – most commonly nuts, sesame seeds, shellfish, cow milk, soy, egg and wheat.
- ❑ **Herbal remedies** – such as Royal Jelly.
- ❑ **Insect stings** – such as bees and wasps. The venom from these insects is different in each case, and therefore allergy to one does not increase the risk of reactions to another.
- ❑ **Latex allergy** – rare, but more common in some people frequently exposed to latex such as health care workers.
- ❑ **Medication** – particularly antibiotics and sometimes x-ray contrast dyes.

SIGNS AND SYMPTOMS

The most noticeable signs and symptoms are:

- ○ hives
- ○ swelling of the throat, lips, tongue, or around the eyes
- ○ difficulty speaking, breathing or swallowing

Other common signs and symptoms may include:

- ○ metallic taste in the mouth
- ○ generalized warmth, flushing, itching, or redness of the skin
- ○ chest discomfort
- ○ abdominal cramps, nausea, vomiting, or diarrhoea
- ○ increased heart rate
- ○ sudden feeling of dizziness or weakness
- ○ anxiety or a sense of doom
- ○ collapse
- ○ loss of consciousness

CARE AND TREATMENT

- ✔ put on disposable gloves if available
- ☽ call **'999'** for an ambulance
- ✔ reassurance
- ✔ adrenaline is the only drug that will act fast enough to rescue someone from a life-threatening reaction
- ✔ casualties who have a history of anaphylaxis are often prescribed self-administered adrenaline using an EpiPen® or Anapen®. If this is the case **assist** the casualty to self-administer their EpiPen® or Anapen® adrenaline.

- remove the injector from the packaging
- remove the safety cap

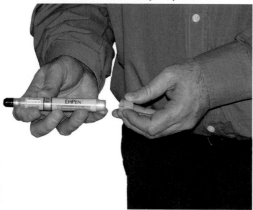

✔ EpiPen®
- hold the EpiPen® 10cm away from the outer thigh

- black tip pointed towards the outer thigh
- jab firmly into the muscle of the thigh. There is no need to remove clothing
- hold firmly in place for 10 seconds
- discard the unit safely
- massage injection site for 10 seconds

✔ Anapen®
- remove black safety cap
- hold Anapen® against outer thigh and press red firing button. There is no need to remove clothing
- black tip pointed towards the outer thigh
- jab firmly into the muscle of the thigh. There is no need to remove clothing
- hold firmly in place for 10 seconds
- discard the unit safely
- massage injection site for 10 seconds

Observe casualty for relapse as severe symptoms sometimes recur after apparent recovery

Useful Resource

The Anaphylaxis Campaign
- ☎ 01252 542029
- http://www.anaphylaxis.org.uk

ASTHMA

Over 1,400 die from asthma in the UK each year, and many of these deaths may be preventable.

Asthma sufferers have very sensitive airways, and when they are exposed to certain triggers, their airways narrow making it difficult for them to breathe.

An asthma attack can take anything from a few minutes to a few days to develop.

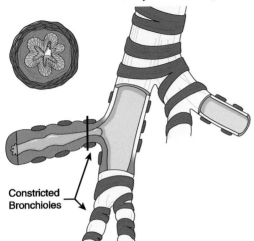

Constricted Bronchioles

There are three main factors that cause airways to become narrow:

1. The inside lining of the airways becomes red and swollen (inflamed)
2. The muscle around the airways constrict (tighten)
3. Extra mucus may be produced

Trigger factors for asthma may include:

❏ Colds and flu
❏ Exposure to known allergens, eg dust mite, pollens, animal dander, moulds
❏ Exposure to chemicals or other occupational sensitisers
❏ Exposure to irritants eg cigarette smoke, perfume
❏ Reflux
❏ Drugs eg aspirin and beta-blockers
❏ Foods eg nuts, seafood
❏ Food additives – colourings, monosodium glutamate (msg)
❏ Changes in weather,
❏ Exercise
❏ Emotion

Asthma is usually considered in three classifications of severity.

Classifications of Asthma Severity			
Severity	**Mild**	**Moderate**	**Severe & Life-threatening**
Symptoms			
Physical exhaustion	No	No	Yes May have paradoxical chest wall movement
Talks in	Sentences	Phrases	Words
Pulse rate	<100/min	<100-120/min	>120/min
Central cyanosis	Absent	May be present	Likely to be present
Wheeze intensity	Variable	Moderate – Loud	Often quiet

SIGNS AND SYMPTOMS

- pale, cool, clammy skin
- coughing, especially at night
- shortness of breath – using all the chest and diaphragm muscles to breathe
- 'sucking in' of the throat and rib muscles
- Severe chest tightness
- wheezing – a high pitched raspy sound
- cyanosis around the lips (bluish colour)
- anxiety and distress
- exhaustion
- rapid, weak pulse
- little or no improvement after using reliever medication
- severe asthma attack: collapse – leading to eventual respiratory arrest

✚ CARE AND TREATMENT

- ✔ sit the casualty comfortably upright
- ✔ be calm and reassuring
- ✔ shake inhaler
- ✔ insert mouthpiece into spacer if available
- ✔ encourage casualty to use inhaler
- ✔ ask the casualty to breathe in and out slowly and deeply after each puff

- ✔ wait 3 minutes. If there is little or no improvement, repeat the above sequence
- ✔ if still no improvement after 5 minutes
  - ☎ call '**999**' for an ambulance

Useful Resources
The National Asthma Campaign
☎ 020 7226 2260 or 0131 226 2544
http://www.asthma.org.uk

CROUP AND EPIGLOTTITIS

Croup is a viral infection of the voice box and windpipe and epiglottitis is a bacterial infection of the epiglottis, the 'flap'-like valve that guards the airway.

Both croup and epiglottitis are conditions that mainly affect children.

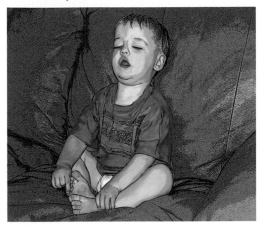

Croup

The onset of croup is slow, usually after another illness, such as a cold or a sore throat. Croup will normally last three to four days and the child may have repeated attacks. Croup is often a mild illness but can get worse quickly, and is often worse at night.

SIGNS AND SYMPTOMS

- ○ appear worse at night
- ○ cold-like symptoms
- ○ hoarse, 'barking' cough (like a seal)
- ○ pale, cool, clammy skin
- ○ may have a slight temperature
- ○ may have breathing difficulty
- ○ may have inspiratory or expiratory stridor (a shrill, harsh sound)

✚ CARE AND TREATMENT

- ✔ reassure the child
- ✔ manage any fevers – the doctor may direct you to give them paracetamol if they have a fever. Follow the instructions on the packet regarding dose
- ✔ give frequent drinks to keep the child well hydrated
- ✔ if there is severe breathing difficulty, or, if the child is distressed, seek medical assistance.
- △ **DO NOT** examine the throat
- △ **DO NOT** use steam as it does not help and may lead to accidental burns

Croup can quickly become serious, so do not hesitate to get medical help. There is effective treatment for severe episodes of croup.

Humidification of the air is often recommended for croup but there is no information to prove that it has any benefits and increases the risk of burns from the hot water or steam.

Epiglottitis

Epiglottitis is usually due to infection by the *Influenza B* bacteria. **It is a life-threatening condition.** It affects children in the two to seven year range with four years the most common age affected.

The infection of the epiglottis causes a gradual obstruction of the airway by the swollen tissue.

 Epiglottitis is an emergency and requires urgent ambulance transport to hospital.

SIGNS AND SYMPTOMS

○ skin often flushed and a high temperature
○ child is quiet, doesn't cough, leans forward and won't talk
○ appears anxious
○ salivary drool, unable to swallow
○ rapid onset over one or two hours
○ child usually has an expiratory 'purr', though other noisy breathing is common

✚ CARE AND TREATMENT

① call **'999'** for an ambulance
✔ reassure the child
✔ keep calm
✔ allow the child to sit in a position of comfort, usually leaning forward and nursed, while in the sitting position, by a parent.
△ **DO NOT** examine the child's throat as this may cause complete blockage

When to seek help

If the child has any of the following, go to a doctor or hospital straight away:

❐ The child's breastbone is drawn in when they take a breath.
❐ The child becomes pale or blue (cyanosed).
❐ The child becomes restless, irritable and/or delirious.
❐ The child has a high temperature and is dribbling.
❐ The child has breathing difficulties.
❐ The child is not drinking enough;
❐ You become concerned for any other reason.

DIABETIC EMERGENCY

Diabetes is a condition which is caused by an imbalance of sugar, or glucose, in the blood. Because all human cells require sugars as food, the body takes in complex sugars in a normal diet. So that the body's cells can use these sugars, an organ called the pancreas secretes a protein hormone called insulin, which attaches to the sugars. This allows the cells to recognise the sugars as food, and absorb the necessary glucose.

Diabetes is due to an imbalance in the production of vital insulin. It is estimated that 3 in every 100 people in the UK have diabetes, and this rate is increasing. Diabetic emergencies appear in two forms *hypoglycaemia* and *hyperglycaemia*.

Hypoglycaemia

Hypoglycaemia, or *low* blood sugar, is a dramatic imbalance where the tissues, especially the brain cells, become starved of essential blood sugar. This condition is the more common type and especially dangerous as its onset is rapid. The result of further deprivation of sugar is that the casualty becomes unconscious and death may follow within hours.

Common causes of low blood sugar levels include:

❐ Drinking alcohol without food
❐ Skipping or delaying meals and snacks
❐ Not eating enough carbohydrate (starchy) food
❐ Too much insulin or diabetes tablets
❐ Extra physical activity without eating extra food

Hyperglycaemia

Hyperglycaemia, or *high* blood sugar, is an imbalance of blood sugar, which usually requires the affected person to supplement their insulin requirements by periodic injections of the hormone. A casualty who

is unable to obtain this supplement is liable to collapse into a serious state called diabetic coma. This condition can develop over many hours or days.

Common causes of high blood sugar levels include:

- ❒ Sickness or Infection
- ❒ Stress
- ❒ Too much carbohydrate (starchy) food at once
- ❒ Not enough insulin or diabetes tablets
- ❒ Other tablets or medicines

 SIGNS AND SYMPTOMS

Low Blood Sugar
- ○ pale
- ○ profuse sweating
- ○ hunger
- ○ dizziness
- ○ tingling around the mouth and lips
- ○ slurred speech

- ○ confused or aggressive – may appear to be drunk
- ○ rapid pulse
- ○ shaking or seizures
- ○ tiredness or weakness
- ○ drowsiness which may lead to becoming unconscious

➕ CARE AND TREATMENT

- ☽ call *'999'* for an ambulance
- ✔ if conscious:
    - ☛ 5 sweets (barley sugar or similar), or
    - ☛ 3 glucose tablets, or
    - ☛ small glass of soft drink (not diet), or
    - ☛ small glass of fruit juice (not squash), or
    - ☛ 100ml of Lucozade
- ✔ repeat if casualty does not improve after 5 -10 minutes
- ✔ on recovery, assist with medication and encourage ingestion of carbohydrate (starchy) food such as a piece of fruit, a bowl of cereal, a sandwich or 2 – 4 dry biscuits

- ✔ if unconscious:
    - ☽ call *'999'* for an ambulance
    - ☛ place casualty in recovery position
- △ **DO NOT** attempt to give insulin injection
- △ **DO NOT** give any food or drink by mouth to an unconscious diabetic

SIGNS AND SYMPTOMS

HIGH BLOOD SUGAR

- ○ hot, dry skin
- ○ feeling constantly thirsty
- ○ passing large volumes of urine, frequently
- ○ smell of acetone (nail polish remover) on the breath
- ○ blurred vision
- ○ weight loss
- ○ infections
- ○ drowsiness progressing to unconsciousness,

CARE AND TREATMENT

- ✔ definitive treatment for high blood sugar requires medical expertise
  - ☽ call **'999'** for an ambulance

Useful Resources

Diabetes UK

☽ 020 7424 1000

http://www.diabetes.org.uk

DROWNING

Drowning occurs after experiencing respiratory impairment from submersion/immersion in liquid which causes a lack of oxygen for the casualty. Drowning is a common cause of accidental death.

The most important consideration the first aid provider can make is to ensure **safety**. Do not attempt a rescue beyond your capabilities.

Immediate resuscitation at the scene is essential for survival of the casualty after drowning. This requires immediate CPR and calling **999** for an ambulance.

Whenever possible, attempt to save the drowning casualty without entry into the water. If entry into the water is essential, take a buoyant rescue aid or flotation device.

Remove all drowning casualties from water by the fastest and safest means available and begin resuscitation as quickly as possible. Use a rescue aid, rope or buoyant aid if the casualty is close to dry land. Use a boat or other water vehicle if possible.

 SIGNS AND SYMPTOMS

- ○ pale, cool skin
- ○ absent, rapid or laboured respirations
- ○ decreased level of consciousness
- ○ coughing
- ○ cyanosis (bluish colour)
- ○ may have rapid, weak, slow or absent pulse

CARE AND TREATMENT

- ☎ call **'999'** for an ambulance
- ✔ check airway and breathing
- ✔ give rescue breaths if safe to do so
- ✔ commence immediate CPR if required
- ✔ place in recovery position once breathing is restored
- ✔ treat hypothermia if present
- ✔ suspect and treat spinal injuries
- △ **DO NOT** attempt a rescue beyond your capabilities

It should be remembered that drowning has a detrimental effect on the respiratory system and recovery, since the drowned casualty may experience a buildup of fluid in the lungs.

All casualty's that have had a drowning experience should seek immediate medical attention.

ⓘ *Untrained rescuers should not attempt to perform any form of resuscitation with a casualty in deep water.*

EPILEPSY

Epilepsy is a disruption of brain function that interrupts the normal electrical activity of the brain. Normally, neurons, which are cells that carry electrical impulses, allow communication between the brain and rest of the body. In epileptics, neurons 'fire' or send electrical impulses toward surrounding cells, stimulating neighbouring cells to fire at one time, causing an 'electrical storm' within the brain, which results in physical changes called seizures or 'fits'. It is only when there is a tendency to have recurrent seizures that epilepsy is diagnosed.

In 70 percent of all cases the cause of epilepsy cannot be identified. Head injuries, strokes, brain tumours, infections such as meningitis, lead poisoning or injury during childbirth mostly cause the remaining 30 percent. There are many different types of seizures.

The main types of seizures are:

- ❏ Tonic-clonic seizures
- ❏ Absence seizures
- ❏ Complex partial seizures
- ❏ Simple partial seizures
- ❏ Atonic seizures
- ❏ Myoclonic seizures

Convulsive seizures

❏ Tonic-clonic seizures are convulsive seizures where the body stiffens (tonic phase) followed by general muscle jerking (clonic phase), and involves the whole brain. The person loses consciousness, their body stiffens and limbs jerk. These seizures generally last up to three minutes. After the seizure the person may want to sleep, or they may have a headache or be confused and disoriented. The person may experience an 'aura' which can precede a tonic-clonic seizure, and this may act as a warning giving the person time to seek a safe place before losing consciousness.

Non-convulsive seizures

❏ An absence seizure causes the person to lose contact with their surroundings for about 30 seconds, with little or no outward sign that anything is wrong. This type of seizure mainly occurs in children and is often mistaken for daydreaming or lack of concentration.

❏ A complex partial seizure is accompanied by impaired consciousness and recall. It may also involve staring, automatic behaviour such as lip smacking, chewing, mumbling, walking, grunting, or the repetition of words or phrases. The person may experience an 'aura' which can precede a complex partial seizure.

❏ A simple partial seizure produces a sudden shock-like jolt to one or more muscles which increases muscle tone and causes movement. These sudden jerks are like those that occur in healthy people as they fall asleep.

❏ A atonic seizure produces a sudden loss of muscle control causing the person to fall to the ground.

❏ A myoclonic seizure produces short forceful jerks that can affect the whole body or just part of it. The jerking can be enough to make the person fall.

 CARE AND TREATMENT

TONIC-CLONIC SEIZURES

✔ protect from harm
✔ place something soft under head

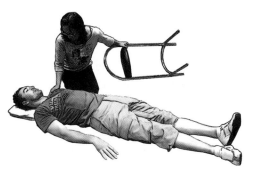

✔ loosen tight clothing and any tie
✔ look for an epilepsy identity card or identity jewellery
✔ roll into recovery position when jerking stops, or immediately if vomited
✔ reassure until fully recovered
✔ remain with the person until recovery is complete

△ **DO NOT** put anything in the casualty's mouth

△ **DO NOT** give them anything to eat or drink until they are fully recovered

△ **DO NOT** restrain the casualty

△ **DO NOT** move the person unless they are in danger

Restraining a person having a seizure may cause musculoskeletal or soft-tissue injury.

If seizure occurs while the person is seated and strapped in, leave them seated until the seizure is finished. Support their head and neck during the seizure. After the seizure place in the recovery position if unconscious, or if there is food, water or vomit in their mouth.

OTHER SEIZURES

✔ protect from harm

✔ look for an epilepsy identity card or identity jewellery

✔ reassure until fully recovered

✔ remain with the person until recovery is complete

✔ explain anything that they may have missed during the seizure

△ **DO NOT** put anything in the casualty's mouth

△ **DO NOT** give them anything to eat or drink until they are fully recovered

△ **DO NOT** restrain the casualty

△ **DO NOT** move the person unless they are in danger

One problem encountered by the first aid provider is that of the well meaning, but untrained, bystander. This person may insist that the epileptic's tongue should be held before they 'swallow it'.

The bystander should be discouraged from actively pulling the casualty's tongue out, or placing anything in the casualty's mouth.

Most epileptics understand what happened to them, and as soon as they recover sufficiently, they continue on with their business. They do not usually require ambulance care and may become upset when one is called.

However, as the first aid provider, you must satisfy yourself that the person is recovering normally, and that there appear to be no complications.

Febrile convulsions

Febrile convulsions occur when a child has a high temperature. The growing brains of small children are more sensitive to fever than are more mature brains, and when the normal brain activity is upset a convulsion or 'fit' can occur.

Febrile convulsions are common and approximately three per cent of children aged six months to six years may have a convulsion when they have a high temperature. Thirty percent of children who have a febrile convulsion will have another episode.

Most children have a body temperature around 37° Celsius. You can take a child's temperature by placing the bulb of the thermometer under their armpit for three minutes with the arm held against their side.

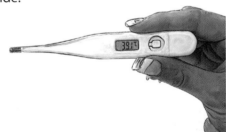

The seizure affects not only the child, but also parents and bystanders who may not have observed this phenomenon before. As a first aid provider, it is part of your responsibility to reassure the witnesses. The greatest fear parents have is that the child is not breathing, and they think that death is imminent.

SIGNS AND SYMPTOMS

- ○ previous history of infection
- ○ child is usually quiet, and appears sick
- ○ flushed, hot skin
- ○ eyes 'roll back'
- ○ have difficulty breathing
- ○ display jerking or twitching movements
- ○ may become stiff or floppy
- ○ child begins convulsing
- ○ salivary drool
- ○ may become 'blue'
- ○ after one to three minutes, child begins breathing normally
- ○ recovers, starts crying
- ○ become unconscious or unaware of their surroundings

CARE AND TREATMENT

For Child
- ✔ remain calm
- ✔ protect child from harm
- ✔ place something soft under head
- ✔ loosen tight clothing
- ✔ roll into recovery position when jerking stops or immediately if vomited
- ✔ reassure until fully recovered
- ✔ remove any excessive clothing
- ✔ on recovery, assess child's breathing – IF NOT BREATHING: rescue breaths

- △ **DO NOT** put anything in the child's mouth
- △ **DO NOT** restrain the child

For Parents/Bystanders
- ✔ reassure
- ✔ arrange to see the local doctor/general practitioner after the convulsion has stopped
- △ discourage removal of child by persons other than ambulance personnel or trained medical assistance

When to call for an ambulance

- ❐ The seizure lasts longer than 5 minutes
- ❐ Another seizure follows quickly
- ❐ It is the first known seizure
- ❐ The person has been injured
- ❐ The person has breathing difficulties after the jerking stops
- ❐ You believe the person needs urgent medical attention
- ❐ The child has difficulty breathing
- ❐ The child looks particularly unwell

Useful Resource
Epilepsy Association
- ☎ 0808 800 5050
- http://www.epilepsy.org.uk

FAINTING

Fainting occurs when the blood supply to the brain is momentarily inadequate, causing a brief loss of consciousness. Fainting is usually caused by a relatively minor event such as the sight of blood, or just prior to receiving an injection.

Fainting can have no medical significance, or the cause can be a serious disorder. Therefore, treat loss of consciousness as a medical emergency until the signs and symptoms are relieved and the cause is known.

There are many causes of fainting, including:

❑ Standing for long periods
❑ The sight of needles
❑ The sight of blood
❑ Pain
❑ Emotional events
❑ Heat

SIGNS AND SYMPTOMS

○ dizziness or feeling light headed
○ nausea
○ pale, cool and clammy skin
○ anxious
○ collapse
○ loss of consciousness
○ rapid recovery after being laid flat

✚ CARE AND TREATMENT

SIMPLE FAINT

✔ if unconscious – recovery position
✔ raise the legs if possible
✔ if conscious – lay the casualty flat and raise the legs if possible

☉ if not fully recovered in a few minu... call **'999'** for an ambulance
✔ if the casualty was injured in the fa... treat any injuries appropriately

HEAT RELATED FAINTING

✔ recovery position
✔ cool casualty by fanning
✔ loosen and remove excessive clothing

HEART CONDITIONS

ardiovascular disease is a term which describes disease to the heart and blood essels, including stroke. According to the British Heart Foundation, cardiovascular disease is the leading cause of death in the UK, accounting for 40% of all deaths.

The heart is a muscular pump, approximately the same size as its owner's fist, and is located behind and slightly to the left of the breastbone. The heart pumps blood to all parts of the body. The blood provides the body with the oxygen and nourishment it needs to function. Waste products carried by the blood are removed from the body by the kidneys and lungs.

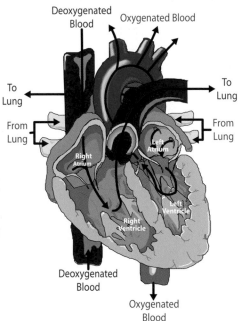

The body contains about five litres of blood which passes through the heart about every minute. But when necessary, such as when exercising, the heart can pump up to four times that amount per minute.

A network of blood vessels carries the blood pumped by the heart around the body. The heart and blood vessels together make up your circulatory system.

Due to factors such as lack of exercise, poor diet, advanced age, and chronic disease, the heart is sometimes compromised, and serious cardiac conditions develop. The four major conditions are: angina, heart attack, heart failure, and cardiac arrest.

CHEST PAIN

Chest pain can be one of the most difficult observations to make as every person has a different 'pain threshold'. Always ask open questions such as "can you describe your pain to me", not "does your pain feel sharp".

Pain can be described as squeezing, crushing, vice-like, heavy, dull, sharp, pressure and many others. Cardiac pain is usually in the centre of the chest, or behind the breastbone. The pain may spread or radiate to the shoulders, neck, jaw and/or arms.

Heart attack

A *heart attack* occurs when a coronary artery is suddenly blocked by a blood clot and the part of the heart muscle supplied by that artery is damaged due to lack of oxygen.

Also known as a **coronary occlusion or myocardial infarction**, a *heart attack* can occur at any time, at any age.

Severe indigestion symptoms which are not relieved by medication may be a heart attack.

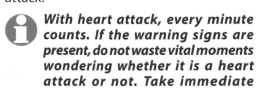 *With heart attack, every minute counts. If the warning signs are present, do not waste vital moments wondering whether it is a heart attack or not. Take immediate action!*

Fatty deposits called plaque build up inside blood vessels and reduce the blood flow. In some cases the plaque builds up so that the vessel is blocked completely. Reduced blood flow can also allow a clot to form and the clot blocks the vessel. When a blockage occurs, oxygen is not delivered to the heart and part of the heart muscle dies. Blockage can occur in one or several coronary arteries.

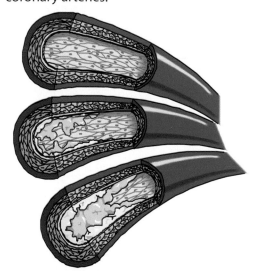

Certain people are at greater risk, due to factors such as hereditary influence, lack of exercise, smoking, poor diet, and high blood pressure. Urgent medical attention is vital.

SIGNS AND SYMPTOMS

○ pale, cool skin
○ chest pain or discomfort, usually in the centre of the chest, may spread or radiate to the shoulders, neck, jaw and/or arms
○ discomfort or pain is similar to angina but is normally more severe
○ sweating
○ light-headedness
○ rapid, irregular, or weak pulse
○ rapid, shallow respirations, or difficulty breathing
○ nausea and/or vomiting
○ symptoms are not completely relieved by resting or by using a nitrate tablet or spray
○ collapse

CARE AND TREATMENT

① call **'999'** for an ambulance
✔ rest the casualty in a position of comfort, usually sitting
✔ assist the casualty to take their medication (nitrate tablets or spray)
✔ reassurance
✔ monitor vital signs

Angina

Angina is a condition caused by constriction of the blood vessels supplying the heart muscle with blood. The chest pain or discomfort is due to a reduction of blood supply to the heart muscle which causes a lack of oxygen to the heart muscle.

Angina has very similar signs and symptoms to a heart attack. Some casualties do not feel 'pain', just an unpleasant sensation or discomfort in the chest.

Angina will usually occur when the heart has to work harder than normal, such as during exercise, or in response to stress. It does not occur all the time because the blood supply, although reduced, is usually able to keep up with the heart's normal demands.

Angina is usually relieved by rest. When rest alone does not bring rapid or effective relief then the use of nitrate tablets or spray is often needed. The pain or discomfort is usually relieved within a couple of minutes, however, if the signs and symptoms last more than 10 to 15 minutes, an ambulance should be called immediately, and the casualty treated for heart attack.

 SIGNS AND SYMPTOMS

Angina and heart attack have very similar signs and symptoms. If in doubt treat as heart attack.

- ○ pale, cool skin
- ○ chest pain or discomfort, usually in the centre of the chest, may spread or radiate to the shoulders, neck, jaw and/or arms
- ○ onset normally with physical activity or emotional upset
- ○ sweating
- ○ rapid, irregular, or weak pulse
- ○ breathlessness
- ○ symptoms usually fade within 15 minutes

➕ CARE AND TREATMENT

- ✔ reassure and rest the casualty in a position of comfort, usually sitting
- ✔ assist the casualty to take their medication
- ✔ monitor vital signs

- ✔ if in doubt if angina or heart attack, treat as heart attack
- ☽ call **'999'** for an ambulance if heaviness or tightness is still present after 15 minutes

Heart failure

Heart failure occurs when the heart is unable to perform its proper function, blood and fluid collects around the lungs and in the body. The casualty finds it difficult to breathe and swelling of the ankles and legs occurs as fluid pools in the extremities.

 SIGNS AND SYMPTOMS

- ○ pale, cold, clammy skin
- ○ chest discomfort, difficulty breathing
- ○ 'bubbly', gasping breaths
- ○ frothy sputum
- ○ swelling of the extremities, especially the ankles, which may show 'dimples'

 CARE AND TREATMENT

- ☽ call **'999'** for an ambulance
- ✔ rest, position of comfort, usually sitting
- ✔ reassurance
- △ **DO NOT** elevate legs

Useful Resource
British Heart Foundation
- ☽ 08450 70 80 70
- http://www.bhf.org.uk

HYPERVENTILATION

Hyperventilation is over-breathing, breathing more than is necessary to meet the body's requirements. Excessive breathing leads to low levels of carbon dioxide in the blood, which causes many of the symptoms that occur in hyperventilation. This reduced level of carbon dioxide causes the arteries to constrict, reducing the flow of blood throughout the body. When this occurs, the brain and body will experience a shortage of oxygen.

Hyperventilation may occur due to a number of causes, often related to anxiety, fear or irrational emotional outbursts. Over-breathing is a perfectly normal reaction to any stressful situation. Generally, when the event has passed, breathing will return to a normal rate.

Sometimes, as a result of prolonged stress or a physical trigger, a continual pattern of over-breathing can occur, whereby the breathing pattern does not return to a normal level.

Reassuring the casualty and a calm approach often quickly relieves the condition.

SIGNS AND SYMPTOMS

○ rapid deep respirations
○ rapid pulse
○ a feeling of shortness of breath
○ pressure, tightness or pain across the chest
○ anxiety
○ dry mouth
○ blurred vision
○ In extreme cases which have continued for some time
  ⊃ 'tingling' in fingers and toes
  ⊃ hand and finger spasms and pain
  ⊃ fainting

CARE AND TREATMENT

✔ reassurance
✔ remove the cause of anxiety, if possible
✔ if fainted, lay casualty flat with legs elevated
☽ call **'999'** for an ambulance if no improvement

Not every casualty who is breathing rapidly is suffering from hyperventilation due to anxiety. In some cases the rapid respirations may be a sign of another, more serious, medical condition. It is important to eliminate more serious causes of rapid breathing, such as asthma.

Re-breathing into a paper bag is not recommended. Deaths have occurred in patients with heart conditions, pneumothorax, or pulmonary embolism mis-diagnosed as hyperventilation and treated with paper bag re-breathing.

MENINGITIS

Meningitis is a term used to indicate inflammation of the thin membrane that covers the brain and spinal cord. There is a fluid between the meninges and the brain and spinal cord called cerebrospinal fluid (CSF), which becomes infected.

Meningitis is mainly due to infection by either viruses or bacteria. Much rarer causes include fungi or cancer cells.

In general, meningitis due to bacteria is more severe than meningitis caused by viruses. Most children with viral meningitis recover completely. However, some children with bacterial meningitis may develop long-term problems, but this depends on the bacterium involved and the age of the child.

 SIGNS AND SYMPTOMS

Early

- severe leg pain - (child cannot stand or walk)
- cold hands or feet when fever present
- pale skin, possibly blue around the lips

Other

- high fever (39⁰c or greater)
- sweating
- chills
- severe headache
- irritability
- eyes sensitive to light
- stiff neck
- loss of appetite
- vomiting
- drowsiness or irritability
- confusion
- lethargy
- may have sore throat
- may have red skin rash
- convulsions
- unconscious

Should your child exhibit some of these signs and symptoms, and you are suspicious of their ability to respond appropriately, take the child to hospital.

If the child is feverish, vomiting and drowsy, *call an ambulance*. Remember that meningitis involves hospitalisation, so the earlier you contact the experts, the better.

Bacterial meningitis can be treated with antibiotics, and most children recover. Viral meningitis usually gets better on its own. Most healthy children and adults with viral meningitis make a complete recovery without long-term problems unless they also have encephalitis.

Meningococcal infection

Meningococcus is a bacteria which invades the bloodstream causing septicaemia. It can also invade the lining of the brain called meningitis.

Children or young adults with meningococcal septicaemia are very ill, have a high fever and may develop a red or purple rash that looks like purple dots or bruises.

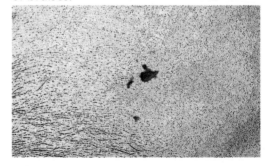

A useful test for the rash is called the tumbler test. Press a glass tumbler firmly against the rash. If the marks stay the same colour and do not fade, then get help immediately.

 SIGNS AND SYMPTOMS

○ red or purple rash that looks like purple dots or bruises that does not disappear when a glass is pressed against it
○ eyes sensitive to light
○ stiff neck
○ high fever (39°c or greater)
○ irritability
○ diarrhoea
○ vomiting
○ loss of appetite
○ drowsiness or irritability
○ confusion
○ lethargy
○ may have sore throat
○ convulsions
○ unconscious

✚ CARE AND TREATMENT

✔ seek urgent medical attention

Some vaccines for meningococcal infection are available, but they do not protect against all types of meningococci.

Pneumococcal disease

Pneumococcal disease refers to a range of illnesses that affect various parts of the body and are caused by infection with the bacterium Streptococcus pneumoniae, commonly known as the pneumococcus.

Illnesses range from mild infections to pneumonia and life-threatening infections of the bloodstream and central nervous system, such as meningitis.

Infection with the pneumococcus bacterium can cause:

❏ Inflammation of the middle ear and ear drum or
❏ Inflammation of one or more sinuses
❏ Pneumonia
❏ Bacteraemia (presence of bacteria in the bloodstream)
❏ Meningitis

The symptoms for pneumococcal disease are not the same as meningococcal disease and a skin rash is NOT common.

SIGNS AND SYMPTOMS

○ breathing difficulties
○ chest pain
○ cough
○ diarrhoea
○ ear pain, especially in children under 3 years old after they have had a cold
○ fever
○ headache
○ lack of appetite
○ low energy
○ nausea
○ neck stiffness
○ reduced hearing
○ vomiting

Treatment can include medications to relieve pain, fluids to treat and avoid dehydration, and rest.

Two vaccines are available for use in the most common strains.

Useful Resource
Meningitis Research Foundation
☎ 080 8800 3344
http://www.meningitis.org

POISONING

Poisons are substances that if inhaled, ingested, absorbed or injected, harm the structures or functions of the body. Some types of poisons may act immediately on the body, others may act more slowly. Some poisons, such as cyanide, are so toxic they only require a tiny amount to be harmful, while others, such as garden sprays, are cumulative and require exposure over a long period to achieve the same level of toxicity. Some may be carcinogenic, and cause fatal cancers some years after exposure.

ⓘ *Whatever the substance, remember that Prevention Is Better Than Cure!*

How to prevent poisoning

- ❏ Store medicines, chemicals and household products safely out of reach and out of sight of children, up high (at least 1.5m) in a locked or child resistant cupboard.
- ❏ **DO NOT** take other people's medicines.
- ❏ Separate medicines from household products.
- ❏ Use medicines and chemicals safely. Be sure that all products are properly labelled and in their original containers.
- ❏ Clean out your medicine cupboard periodically. Take out-of-date medicines to a pharmacy for disposal.
- ❏ Children tend to mimic adults, so avoid taking medicines in their presence.
- ❏ Refer to medicines by their correct names. They are not sweets or lollies.
- ❏ Use personal protective equipment (PPE) when spraying or painting. Ensure there is adequate ventilation, with circulating air.
- ❏ Take off any contaminated clothing immediately.
- ❏ Keep everything in original containers, never in cups or soft drink bottles, since the original containers will be labelled with the appropriate warnings. Using a different container may give a child the mistaken impression that the product is both safe and drinkable.

If poisoning occurs, obtain a history, look for empty bottles, containers, and sometimes suicide notes. If possible, ascertain what poison or medicine has been taken, including how much and when.

The wide varieties of poisonous substances present with a similarly wide variety of signs and symptoms. The list below is not exhaustive and casualties may present with all, or some of these signs and symptoms.

SIGNS AND SYMPTOMS

May include the following:
- pale, cool, clammy skin
- rapid, weak (sometimes erratic) pulse
- nausea and/or vomiting
- bluish skin colour
- headache
- burns around the mouth
- burning pain in the mouth or throat
- blurred vision
- ringing in the ears
- smell of fumes or odours
- stomach pains or cramps
- drowsiness, which may lead to unconsciousness
- seizures
- breathing difficulties

CARE AND TREATMENT
- ✔ make the area safe by sealing containers or ventilating the area
- ☺ call **'999'** for an ambulance
- ✔ rescue breaths and CPR as required
- ✔ show any containers to the ambulance
- ✔ gather any evidence that may assist in identifying the substance, drug or creature. Give this information to the ambulance crew
- ✔ provide as much information as possible about the poisons when calling for help
- ✔ keep any samples of vomited material
- ✔ always wear protective gloves if available
- ✔ monitor the casualty at all times

Specific treatment

SWALLOWED POISON
- ✔ if conscious, ask the casualty what they have taken
- △ **DO NOT** try to make the patient vomit

POISON ON THE SKIN
- ✔ remove contaminated clothing, taking care to avoid contact with the chemical
- ✔ flood the skin with cool running water for at least 20 minutes

POISON IN THE EYE
- ✔ gently holding the eyelids open, flood the eye inside and out with water from a cup, jug or slowly running tap water for at least 10 minutes
- ✔ cover eye(s) with sterile eye dressing

INHALED POISON
- ✔ get the person to fresh air as quickly as possible if safe to do so.
- ✔ if safe, open doors and windows
- △ **DO NOT** place yourself at risk

INJECTED POISON
- ✔ remove sting if possible
- ✔ apply cold pack

When to call for help

- ❏ If you or someone in your care may have been poisoned
- ❏ **DO NOT** wait for any symptoms to occur before calling for assistance
- ❏ If in doubt call and check

Poisons may include:

- ➲ car products
- ➲ cleaning products
- ➲ insecticides, weed killers, rodent and snail baits
- ➲ kerosene, petrol, methylated spirits, etc.
- ➲ any over-the-counter medicines
- ➲ paints and thinners
- ➲ perfumes and aftershaves
- ➲ plants and mushrooms
- ➲ prescription medicines
- ❏ If a person is bitten or stung by a marine creature, animal, reptile, spider or insect

Useful Resources

NHS Direct

- ➲ 0845 4647 (England/Wales)
- ➲ 08454 25 24 24 (Scotland)

http://www.nhsdirect.nhs.uk

Child Accident Prevention Trust

http://www.capt.org.uk

STROKE

According to the UK Stroke Association, stroke is the third most common cause of death. A stroke is a brain attack and when a person suffers a stroke, essential supplies of blood and oxygen are cut off from the cells in the brain. These control everything we do such as speech, movement and breathing.

 Treat stroke with the same degree of seriousness as a heart attack.

Two common causes prompt strokes:

- ❏ A blocked blood vessel to the brain (an occlusion),
- ❏ A ruptured blood vessel causing bleeding into the brain (intracranial haemorrhage).

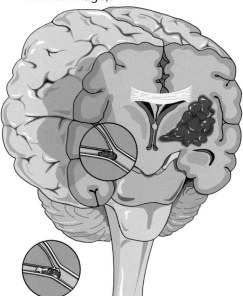

When a stroke occurs, it kills brain cells in the immediate area because they are no longer receiving the oxygen and nutrients needed to function.

Stroke is most common in the elderly, but people of any age and any level of physical fitness can suffer the injury.

Strokes occur in two main forms:

Cerebral Vascular Accident (CVA) which causes permanent damage to the brain tissue through oxygen starvation (blocked vessel), or pressure (bleeding). There is permanent damage to the brain, resulting in physical and/or sensory impairment.

Transient Ischaemic Attack (TIA) sometimes referred to as a 'mini stroke', which is a temporary condition usually caused by a minor blockage of the brain's blood vessels. The blockage lasts long enough to temporarily show the signs and symptoms of a CVA. TIAs may last from several minutes to several hours. Don't ignore TIA's as they can lead to a major stroke and the casualty should seek medical advice.

SIGNS AND SYMPTOMS

- **FAST** - **F**ace **A**rm **S**peech **T**est
    - **F**acial weakness - can the person smile? Has their mouth or eye drooped?
    - **A**rm weakness - can the person raise both arms?
    - **S**peech problems - can the person speak clearly and understand what you say?
    - **T**est all three symptoms
- if the casualty fails any one of the **FAST** tests call **'999'**

Other symptoms

- sudden severe headache
- sudden nausea and/or vomiting
- warm, flushed, clammy skin
- slow, full pulse
- may have distended neck veins
- blurred vision in one or both eyes
- may have unequal pupils
- paralysis, weakness or loss of coordination of limbs, usually on one side of the body
- loss of balance
- difficulty swallowing or salivary drool
- urinary incontinence
- brief loss of consciousness
- unconscious – 'snoring' respirations
- may have seizures

CARE AND TREATMENT

- if the casualty fails any one of the **FAST** tests *act FAST* and call **'999'**
- ✔ adopt position of comfort, taking care that the airway does not become obstructed by drool or mucus
- ✔ reassurance – talk to the casualty even if unconscious
- ✔ recovery position if unconscious, constantly observe
- ✔ maintain body temperature

Prompt action can prevent further damage to the brain and help the casualty make a full recovery. Delays in obtaining treatment can result in death or major long-term disabilities.

Useful Resource
National Stroke Foundation

- 0845 30 33 100
- http://www.stroke.org.uk

5 SPECIAL FIRST AID

- Environmental emergencies
- Bites and stings
- Emergency childbirth
- Sudden Infant Death Syndrome (SIDS)

This chapter covers emergency childbirth and Sudden Infant Death Syndrome (SIDS).

By the end of this section you should be able to:

- Recognise and manage environmental emergencies.
- Identify and treat snake, spider, bee, ant, wasp & sea creature bites and stings.
- Manage the a delivery of a baby in situations where medial assistance is not readily available
- Describe the three ways to reduce the risk of a SIDS emergency.
- Manage a SIDS emergency.

ENVIRONMENTAL CONDITIONS AND EXPOSURE

The human body maintains a temperature between 36-37°c. Any excessive variation to this range has a detrimental effect on body functions. As a general observation, it may be said that the human brain does not react well to excessive body heat, and the heart is sensitive to cold.

The body has some natural defence mechanisms against excessive heat and cold. It regulates body heat by sweating, releasing heat through the body surface (heat loss), and through lung moisture evaporation. Cold is managed by shivering, which generates heat within the body.

Often, environmental influences determine the stability of the human body's temperature. These influences are important in relation to first aid. Heat and cold related conditions may bring on serious functional impairment.

Heat related conditions are those brought on by exposure to high temperatures and humidity. The most spectacular example of a serious heat related problem, is the televised distress suffered by athletes during long distance running events, conducted during hot and humid conditions.

Heat may induce heat cramps, heat exhaustion and/or heat stroke. Less well known are industrial and engine room situations which can mimic tropical conditions while outside temperatures are actually much lower.

Dehydration

Dehydration is a condition caused by the casualty's loss of fluids from perspiration and prolonged exposure to heat and humidity. When the casualty's fluid loss exceeds their input through drinking, dehydration occurs and the blood volume lessens. A prolonged period of dehydration will lead to shock and, in susceptible casualties, such as the frail elderly and very young, this can be fatal.

 SIGNS AND SYMPTOMS

○ pale, cool, clammy skin
○ rapid breathing
○ profuse and prolonged sweating
○ thirst
○ loss of skin elasticity ('pinch test' on back of hand)
○ sunken eyes in children

✚ CARE AND TREATMENT

✔ complete rest in the shade, no further exertion
✔ remove unnecessary clothing
✔ give cool water to drink
✔ ensure casualty has assistance when recovered

Heat cramps

Heat cramps are caused by the loss of complex salts (electrolytes) through an imbalance in the body's fluid requirements – the body is losing more fluids than it is replacing. This debit causes the hard-working muscles to lose their vital electrolyte balance, causing muscular contraction (cramping).

SIGNS AND SYMPTOMS

○ pale, cool, clammy skin
○ rapid breathing
○ profuse and prolonged sweating
○ cramps in the limbs and/or abdomen
○ thirst, nausea and/or vomiting
○ constant headache
○ exhaustion and lethargy

✚ CARE AND TREATMENT

✔ complete rest in the shade, no further exertion
✔ lie casualty down
✔ remove unnecessary clothing
✔ cool casualty by sponging with water
✔ when nausea passes, give cool water to drink (cautiously)
✔ ensure casualty seeks medical assistance when recovered

Heat stroke

This condition is not to be confused with 'sun stroke', the common ailment of headache and nausea suffered by children and careless adults who remain in the sun too long without a hat. Also known as 'Core Temperature Emergency', with a core temperature above 40.6 °c heat stroke is potentially life threatening.

In this condition, the body's temperature regulation centre in the brain has been rendered inoperable, and the body temperature continually rises, causing eventual brain damage. Immediate, active intervention is necessary to avoid coma and death.

SIGNS AND SYMPTOMS

○ pale, clammy skin
○ sweating if associated with exertion
○ cramping pains in the limbs or abdomen
○ nausea
○ uncontrolled spasms of affected limb(s)

✚ CARE AND TREATMENT

✔ rest in the shade
✔ gently stretch the affected muscle
✔ apply ice pack
✔ when nausea passes, give sips of cool water to drink (with caution)
△ avoid massaging affected limb
△ avoid any further exercise

Heat exhaustion

Heat exhaustion is caused by exertion accompanied by heat and high humidity.

SIGNS AND SYMPTOMS

- ◯ flushed, hot, dry skin
- ◯ core temperature 40.6 °c or more
- ◯ the casualty has ceased sweating
- ◯ rapid pulse, gradually weakening
- ◯ irrational or aggressive behaviour
- ◯ staggering gait, fatigue
- ◯ visual disturbances, headache
- ◯ vomiting
- ◯ collapse and seizures
- ◯ coma – death

✚ CARE AND TREATMENT

- ☽ call **'999'** for an ambulance
- ✔ complete rest in shade
- ✔ remove casualty's clothing
- ✔ cool casualty by any means possible – ice packs to neck, groin and armpits
- ✔ cover casualty with wet sheet and keep wet. Fan to increase cooling
- ✔ be prepared to resuscitate as required
- ✔ fluids can be given if casualty is fully conscious

- ✔ if unconscious or semi-conscious, nothing by mouth. Re-hydration is required by intravenous fluids administered by a doctor or ambulance crew

Exposure to cold

Exposure to cold has effects which are no less serious than exposure to heat and humidity. Remember that an elderly person in an unheated house during winter, who is incapacitated and unable to summon assistance, is at risk from exposure to cold and hypothermia.

There are several common situations

where persons suffer from exposure to low temperatures. This includes being caught out in inclement weather during walking, being soaked in cold water and unable to change, and being subject to cold winds

Categories of Hypothermia			
	Mild	**Moderate**	**Severe**
Temperature	32-35 °c	30-32 °c	less than 30 °c
Shivering	Vigorous	Reducing in intensity	Nil
Skin	Pale and cool	Pale and cool	Pale, blue and Cold
Level of consciousness	Apathy, slurred speech	Semi-conscious	Unconscious
Breathing	Normal	Slow	Not able to be detected
Pulse	Slow	Slow	Not able to be detected
Other	Unco-ordinated	Increased muscle rigidity	May appear dead

(wind chill) without proper protection, or not being able to afford adequate heating and clothing.

SIGNS AND SYMPTOMS

- pale, cold skin
- increasing lethargy, drowsiness, lack of muscular co-ordination
- uncommunicative, poor judgement
- shivering

CARE AND TREATMENT

✔ warm slowly by adding additional clothing, heating source, body heat
✔ if wet, change the casualty's clothing if in stable environment
✔ if conscious, give warm, sweet drinks
✔ when able to stand, encourage mild exercise

Hypothermia

Hypothermia occurs when the body's control mechanisms fail to maintain a normal body temperature above 35°c. Hypothermia results from prolonged exposure to cold temperatures.

Factors that commonly increase the risk of hypothermia include advanced or very young age, substance abuse, impaired mental status, or immersion in cold water.

SIGNS AND SYMPTOMS

- pale, cold skin – no capillary return when fingernails are pressed
- slow pulse, sometimes irregular
- slow, shallow respirations
- blurred, or double vision
- casualty is silent, appears asleep, difficult to rouse; may be unconscious
- casualty experiences a sense of 'wellbeing'
- absence of shivering
- if very cold, may have non-reacting pupils and appear 'death-like'

CARE AND TREATMENT

✔ provide shelter from cold, rain, wet ground, and wind
☽ call '999' for an ambulance
✔ warm casualty, wrap in blanket, 'space blanket' or similar. Move to a warm area
✔ remove cold or wet clothing as soon as possible
✔ cover casualties with blankets and keep them out of the wind
✔ once casualty commences shivering, reassess heating
✔ be prepared for sudden collapse and resuscitation
✔ if conscious, give warm, sweet drinks
△ **DO NOT** rub affected area
△ **DO NOT** expose to excessive heat
△ **DO NOT** give alcohol

BITES AND STINGS

Bites and stings are a type of injected poison. As for general poisoning, prevention is better than cure, so take care when in an area frequented by snakes and spiders, and treat venomous sea creatures with respect

Snakes

Envenomation from snake bite is uncommon in the UK. The only indigenous venomous snake is the adder, although exotic snakes are kept as pets. The bite from an adder may cause local and systemic effects. Fatal bites are rare, but the potential for severe envenomation must not be underestimated.

In most cases, the snake strikes swiftly and injects venom below the surface of the skin into the tissues, which is then absorbed by the lymphatic system.

🔍 SIGNS AND SYMPTOMS

- O puncture marks, or parallel scratches on the skin
- O severe pain
- O redness and swelling at the bite site
- O anxiety
- O pale, cool skin with progressive onset of sweating
- O rapid, weak pulse
- O rapid, shallow breathing
- O breathing difficulties
- O blurred vision, drooping eyelids
- O difficulty swallowing and speaking
- O abdominal pain
- O nausea and/or vomiting
- O headache

✚ CARE AND TREATMENT

- ✔ ensure safety
- ✔ reassure and rest the casualty
- ☽ call **'999'** for an ambulance
- ✔ gently wash the bitten area
- ✔ apply a roller bandage starting from over the bite site, and then wind as far up the limb as possible
- ✔ immobilise the limb
- ✔ send any evidence of the snake to the hospital only if safe to do so
- △ avoid elevating the limb
- △ **DO NOT** use an arterial tourniquet
- △ **DO NOT** try to capture the snake
- △ **DO NOT** cut the bitten area
- △ **DO NOT** suck the bitten area

The main treatment for a snake bite is the application of a compression bandage and immobilisation of the limb. This bandage is applied as firmly as bandaging a sprained ankle, and is designed to slow the movement of venom through the lymphatic system which helps to slow or prevent the venom from leaving the bite site.

Spiders and Scorpions

There are no deadly spiders or scorpions indigenous to the UK. Like snakes some exotic species of spiders and scorpions are kept as pets, and these can cause serious illness or death if not treated.

🔍 SIGNS AND SYMPTOMS

- O pain at the site of the bite
- O may be localised redness, swelling and sweating
- O nausea, vomiting and abdominal pain

○ rapid pulse
○ loss of co-ordination
○ tremors and muscle spasms
○ rapid, shallow breathing

✚ CARE AND TREATMENT

✔ reassure
✔ cold compress to relieve pain
✔ monitor vital signs

Ticks

Ticks are small creatures capable of spreading diseases and causing infection. Ticks can be found anywhere on the body, but hairy areas, skin clefts and crevices should be examined carefully.

SIGNS AND SYMPTOMS

○ local irritation
○ lethargy
○ muscle weakness, especially in children
○ unsteady gait
○ double vision
○ difficulty in swallowing or breathing
○ rarely allergic reactions occur:
  ➲ rapid local swelling
  ➲ wheezing and difficulty breathing
  ➲ collapse

Signs and symptoms generally develop over several days but allergic symptoms can occur within hours.

✚ CARE AND TREATMENT

✔ reassure
✔ slide the open blades of sharp pointed tweezers on each side of the tick and lever it upwards

✔ always check the whole body of the casualty, including the ears, skin creases and hair for further ticks
✔ after removal of a tick the casualty should be advised to see a doctor to check that no further treatment is required.
△ avoid squeezing the tick because even slight pressure may inject more venom

Bees

Bee stings for most people is only a temporary irritation. For others however, these stings have the potential to cause death.

The venom associated with bee stings causes a severe allergic reaction in susceptible people, and can cause respiratory and cardiac arrest.

SIGNS AND SYMPTOMS

○ evidence of bee sting with the barb present
○ pain and itching at the site
○ swelling of the stung area
○ in allergic casualties:
  ➲ onset of wheezing and breathing difficulties
  ➲ facial swelling and hives
  ➲ rapid pulse
  ➲ collapse

✚ CARE AND TREATMENT

✔ reassure
✔ remove bee sting by scraping with fingernail or similar
✔ cold compress to reduce swelling and pain
✔ if onset of allergic reaction:

☞ apply a roller bandage starting from over the bite site, and then wind as far up the limb as possible

☞ immobilise the limb

☼ call **'999'** for an ambulance

△ avoid squeezing or touching the barb

Wasps and Hornets

These insects are attracted to aromatic or sweet-tasting things, and will enter food containers such as open soft-drink cans. The creature will then sting when inadvertently handled, and can sting multiple times. Similar to bees, the wasps become aggressive when their nest is disturbed.

 SIGNS AND SYMPTOMS

○ severe pain at the affected site

○ immediate swelling, especially if the throat has been stung

○ breathing difficulties

 CARE AND TREATMENT

✔ reassure

✔ cold compress to reduce swelling and pain

✔ if onset of allergic reaction:

  ☞ apply a roller bandage starting from over the bite site, and then wind as far up the limb as possible

  ☞ immobilise the limb

  ☼ call **'999'** for an ambulance

✔ rescue breaths if respiratory arrest

Sea creatures

Many sea creatures are venomous, and the best way to avoid envenomation is to avoid the creatures. As an example, don't pick up or handle creatures washed up on the beach or in rock pools, and don't swim where Jellyfish or the Portuguese Man-of-War are prevalent.

Jellyfish, Portuguese Man-of-War, sea anemones and corals can cause painful stings. Most deadly marine creatures are generally found in tropical areas.

 SIGNS AND SYMPTOMS

○ immediate severe pain, with irrational behaviour because of the pain

○ rapid, irregular pulse

○ frosted pattern of sting marks

○ collapse

○ respiratory arrest

○ cardiac arrest

✚ CARE AND TREATMENT

✔ reassure

✔ dry cold compress to relieve pain

✔ tropical jellyfish stings

  ☞ apply liberal quantities of vinegar for a minimum of 30 seconds

✔ if onset of allergic reaction:

  ☞ apply a roller bandage starting from over the bite site, and then wind as far up the limb as possible

  ☞ immobilise the limb

  ☼ call **'999'** for an ambulance

MARINE PUNCTURE

Some marine creatures are virtually invisible among rocks and the venomous spines on its back it erects when threatened or stepped on.

If stood on the creatures will cause a puncture wound or leave sharp spines embedded in the soles of the feet.

SIGNS AND SYMPTOMS

- ○ severe pain at the site of envenomation
- ○ swelling
- ○ open wound and/or bleeding
- ○ irrational behaviour
- ○ rapid pulse
- ○ breathing difficulties
- ○ collapse – coma

CARE AND TREATMENT

- ✔ reassure
- ✔ HOT water immersion of the site to relieve pain for at least 30 minutes – ensure that the water will not scald the casualty
- ☾ call **'999'** for an ambulance if the wound is severe or spines are embedded
- △ **DO NOT** bandage the wound

SIGNS AND SYMPTOMS

- ○ pain at the bite site
- ○ swelling
- ○ open wound and/or bleeding
- ○ anxiety

CARE AND TREATMENT

- ✔ reassure
- ✔ put on disposable gloves if available
- ✔ clean the wound with soap and warm water
- ✔ dry area and cover with a sterile dressing if possible
- ✔ control bleeding:
  - ☛ apply direct pressure
  - ☛ raise the injured area
- ✔ the casualty should be taken or sent to hospital

ANIMAL BITES

Bites from animals, especially with sharp pointed teeth, can cause deep puncture wounds that carry germs deep into the tissues of the body. Human bites can also crush the tissues.

Any bite in which the skin is broken requires prompt first aid. Bite wounds are also prone to infection, such as rabies and tetanus, and prompt medical attention is required for all animal bites.

SUSPENSION TRAUMA

Suspension trauma occurs when a person is suspended in an upright position motionlessly, affecting blood circulation. After a fall, the harness holds the worker in an upright position and if left immobile, blood accumulates in the legs, which in turn reduces the amount in circulation.

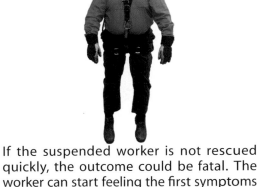

If the suspended worker is not rescued quickly, the outcome could be fatal. The worker can start feeling the first symptoms of shock in as little as three minutes but it is usually between five and twenty minutes. Unconsciousness will occur a few minutes later and then the brain can start to die. Once unconscious and if the body is upright the airway can become obstructed.

SIGNS AND SYMPTOMS

- ○ light headed
- ○ nausea
- ○ breathlessness
- ○ dizziness
- ○ sweating
- ○ paleness
- ○ hot flushes
- ○ "greying" or loss of vision

- ○ unusually low pulse rate usually occurring after the incidence of increased pulse rate
- ○ loss of consciousness

✚ CARE AND TREATMENT

- ⓘ call for help immediately
- ✔ reassure
- ✔ if unconscious
    - ☛ sit the casualty upright with their legs flat
- △ **DO NOT** lie the casualty down
- △ **DO NOT** allow the casualty to:
    - ☛ lay down flat
    - ☛ stand up
    - ☛ exercise
    - ☛ drink or eat
- ✔ if unconscious
    - ☛ manage the airway with the casualty in a sitting position
- ✔ if CPR is required then you must lay them flat and perform CPR

First aid training always advises that all unconscious casualty's are placed into the recovery position. In the case of suspension trauma if you do this they are likely to die.

The first reason for this is due to lack of circulation, blood pools in the legs and builds up toxins. These toxins and the lack of oxygen can cause serious problems to the brain, liver and kidneys.

The second reason is the sudden reflow of blood that can cause excessive blood pressure to the heart. This pressure can cause the heart to fail.

Useful Resource

www.suspensiontrauma.info
www.hse.gov.uk/research/crr
pdf/2002/crr02451.pdf

EMERGENCY CHILDBIRTH

At some time in the future, you may be called on to assist with the birth of a baby. This activity is a most rewarding one for a first aid provider, and there is no need to be frightened or nervous about it. The mother requires support and reassurance more than anything else, and if you appear calm and confident this will show her that you are someone to rely on.

Remember that women have been performing the function of childbirth for a long time, and the process is natural. You are there to provide any help that may be required during a process that is controlled by the mother. Your active intervention is necessary only in extreme situations.

Childbirth is open to infection. It is imperative that you take all possible precautions for mother and child against infection from yourself and from the surroundings.

Ensure that you wear gloves during the process. If gloves are unavailable, ensure that you scrub your hands thoroughly with soap and warm water.

Change your gloves, or scrub your hands each time they come in contact with contaminated material, eg faeces, blood, etc.

Childbirth occurs in three stages:

- ❒ 1st Stage – the onset of labour
- ❒ 2nd Stage – the birth of the baby
- ❒ 3rd Stage – the delivery of the afterbirth

First stage: Onset of labour

The onset of labour may last between 2 and 24 hours. It begins with cramp-like pains in the lower abdomen, a 'heavy' feeling low down near the pubic area, or some may experience back pain. The pains occur regularly every 5-20 minutes, and they last for approximately 30 seconds.

In some instances, examination of the woman's vagina may reveal a 'show' of bloodstained mucus heralding the imminent birth of the baby. At this point, urgent ambulance or medical attention should be sought.

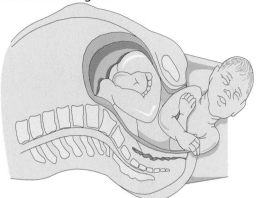

During this stage, there may occur a 'breaking of the waters'; a sudden flow of fluid from the membrane around the baby.

If it is obvious that it is too late to move the woman to hospital, there is little you can do except keep the mother-to-be clean and provide reassurance.

Now that the birthing process has begun, you should prepare for it by organising:

- ✔ a large plastic sheet to cover the bed or floor
- ✔ two or three clean sheets
- ✔ three clean linen or string ties about 25cm long
- ✔ sharp scissors which have been boiled and kept as sterile as possible
- ✔ sterile pads (large combines are ideal) for the mother
- ✔ a warm nappy or 'bunny rug' for the baby
- ✔ towels, face washers and warm water to clean the mother

Second stage: Birth of the baby

At this stage, the baby has moved down further into the birth canal. The pains change to 'bearing down' pains. These contractions may stimulate the mother to want to pass a bowel motion. Do not let her go to the toilet unaccompanied! Check that medical aid is on the way.

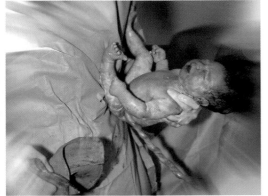

The baby will move down the birth canal. There will usually be an increase in bloodstained mucus, and eventually the top of the baby's head will become visible – this is called 'crowning'. Most babies are born head-first, though occasionally a baby presents buttocks-first. This is known as a 'breech birth', and the mother may be unable to give birth without trained medical assistance.

When you observe the 'crowning' process, if possible again wash your hands or change your gloves if time allows. The mother may unavoidably pass a bowel motion. If this occurs, remove the faeces completely with a pad and cover the stained area.

The mother will be in some pain and have an urge to 'push'. Encourage her not to hold her breath. Help her stay calm and advise her to 'push' when the urge is very strong.

As the baby is gradually pushed through the opening of the birth canal, gently support its head – Do not pull the baby, as

it will be delivered normally in successive contractions.

Should the umbilical cord be wound around the baby's neck, slide two fingers underneath it and gently ease it over the baby's head. There is enough slack in the cord to do this easily.

When the baby's head appears, it will initially face the anus, but as the baby is delivered, it will spontaneously rotate to face one side. This is quite normal.

Support the baby's head until the next contraction, during which the baby's shoulders will appear. At this point, shift your grip to approximately the baby's armpits and gently lift it towards the mother's abdomen as the final contraction expels it entirely from the birth canal. Take note of the time.

Very occasionally, the baby's head is born but the body is delayed (usually by the shoulders), ask the woman to change her position (try all fours or supported squat).

If the baby presents as a breech birth, it will be born body-first. The baby is unlikely to be expelled normally, so you must attempt to avoid the cord from becoming 'pinched' in the birth canal.

Gently pull down a loop of the cord to relieve the pressure. Get medical help urgently!

Care of the newborn infant

The baby will be wet and slippery, and at this stage will cool down rapidly. It is essential that you retain the baby's body heat by wrapping it in a warm cover. Give it to its mother to hold, taking care not to interfere with the cord.

After one minute, if the baby appears not to be breathing, clear the airway and begin resuscitation immediately!

After 2-3 minutes, the cord will stop pulsating. At this point, the baby is no longer dependent on the mother's circulatory system, and is ready to go it alone.

Use the linen or string ties to tie the cord firmly in three places: 10cm, 15cm, and 20cm from the baby's navel. Tie the cords firmly enough to prevent any flow of blood through it which may allow the baby to bleed.

You need not cut the cord if medical help is on the way, but if you are required to do so, cut the cord leaving TWO ties on the baby's side of the separation.

As soon as possible after the delivery, quickly assess the baby, noting the time it was delivered, its colour at birth (blue? dusky? pale?), any deformities or skin discolouration, strength of cry (loud and lusty, or weak), and whether the baby moves spontaneously, or just lies still. This is important information for the baby's subsequent medical examination. Repeat the examination after 5-10 minutes and note any changes. Keep the baby under constant observation.

Third stage: Delivery of the afterbirth (placenta)

The afterbirth, or placenta, was the source of the baby's blood supply in the uterus. With no further use, it will be expelled through the birth canal by contractions, similar to the birth of the baby.

This usually occurs 15-60 minutes after the baby's birth. During this time it is essential that you **DO NOT** apply pressure, or strain, on the cord or touch the mother's abdomen.

To encourage delivery of the placenta, ensure that the mother raises and parts her legs slightly. Put the baby on the mother's breast, as this will stimulate the uterus to contract and slow any bleeding. The placenta will be delivered by successive contractions.

After delivery, it is important that the placenta is retained for examination by a medical professional.

Care of the mother

Wash the mother and place dressing combines or sanitary pads in place. Take her pulse, assess her colour and check carefully for any further bleeding and what you may consider to be excessive blood loss. Provided she is conscious and not ill or drowsy, give her warm, sweet drinks and encourage her to rest. Keep her under constant observation.

Retain all bloodstained towels and pads for medical examination.

If requested by the mother, assist her with cleaning herself up and in changing her clothing.

SUDDEN INFANT DEATH SYNDROME (SIDS)

SIDS or Cot Death, is defined as "The sudden and unexpected death of an infant under 1 year of age, with onset of the lethal episode apparently occurring during sleep, that remains unexplained after a thorough investigation including performance of a complete autopsy, and review of the circumstances of death and the clinical history. SIDS occurs in infants usually in the one to twelve month age group.

A great deal of research has been carried out on SIDS and, although no sure method of prevention has been discovered, experts have devised a list of risk factors. According to The Foundation for the Study of Infant Deaths, since the *Reducing the Risk of SIDS* program was first launched in the UK in 1991, cot deaths have reduced by 75%.

Three ways to *reduce the risk of sids*:

1. Put the baby on the back to sleep. The risk of SIDS is increased if babies sleep on their belly or side. Babies are best placed on their backs to sleep.

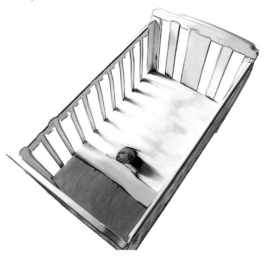

2. Make sure the baby's head remains uncovered during sleep. If a baby's head becomes covered during sleep the risk of SIDS is increased. Loose bedding material can cover the baby's head, so ensure that you securely tuck the baby in so that they can not slip under the bedclothes. Consideration should be given to:

   ✔ making sure the baby's head remains uncovered during sleep

   ✔ not putting the baby on a water bed or bean bag

   ✔ taking a baby into an adult bed may be unsafe.

   ✔ the baby may get caught under the bedding or pillows,

   ✔ become trapped between the wall and the bed,

   ✔ fall out of bed

   ✔ be rolled on by someone who sleeps very deeply or who has taken medicine, drugs or alcohol that can cause them to sleep heavily.

   ✔ placing the baby on the back to sleep

   ✔ using a firm, clean, well-fitting mattress

   ✔ tucking in the baby's bedclothes securely

   ✔ positioning the baby's feet at the bottom of the cot.

   ✔ not using quilts, doonas, duvets, pillows, soft toys and cot bumpers in the cot.

3. Keep the baby smoke free, before and after birth.

   The risk of SIDS is increased if the mother smokes during pregnancy. There is also some evidence to suggest that if fathers smoke while the mother is pregnant the risk of SIDS is increased.

A SIDS death affects all who are involved. Parents and near relatives become distraught, especially as there appears no reason for the death. Friends and neighbours are also affected, and the attending ambulance crew, police and medical staff are not unaffected. It is a highly emotional incident, and as a first aid provider, perhaps with initial contact, you are also at risk of emotional involvement. It is difficult, but you will be expected to provide support for others, and your objectivity may be tested.

SIGNS AND SYMPTOMS

○ no signs of circulation
  ⊃ unconscious
  ⊃ absent respirations
  ⊃ absent pulse
○ cyanosis (bluish colour)

CARE AND TREATMENT

✔ quickly and carefully examine the infant
✔ if in doubt, ATTEMPT RESUSCITATION
✔ leave the infant as found, avoid disturbing bedclothes
✔ contact ambulance and advise 'suspected SIDS'
✔ comfort parent(s), assist in obtaining support, relatives, etc
✔ remain on scene until police arrive and provide information

Police become involved in an unexpected death automatically as it becomes the subject of a Coroner's Investigation. The attending police officers will advise the child's parents of all necessary formalities.

The police offices are not there to indicate or attribute blame.

If you are unfortunate enough to become involved in a SIDS case, you have been involved 'at the sharp end'. Although you may not think so, you have been emotionally affected. Ensure that you talk the incident through with somebody, especially with someone who will understand. If you don't know anyone close with whom you may wish to share your feelings, contact the ambulance crew who attended. They will be only too willing to share it with you – they understand your feelings and know what an emotional trial it has been.

For more information, contact SIDS and Kids for written material, support or advice.

Useful Resource
The Foundation for the Study of Infant Deaths
  ☎ **0870 787 0554**
http://www.sids.org.uk/fsid/

MANUAL HANDLING INJURIES

Back injuries cost the Australian taxpayer, and commercial and industrial interests, many millions of dollars annually. Initial medical costs, and the cost of prolonged rehabilitation of back injury patients, account for the major proportion of industrial insurance payouts. As well as being an expensive injury, an injured back is painful and debilitating. In most cases, the injury was preventable.

The spinal column is a series of interconnected bones, separated by cartilage shock absorbers. Although the spine is flexible, it is not designed to withstand abnormal flexion under load. Lifting weights and carrying loads are normal functions for active humans, however, care must be taken not to exceed the ability of the spine to adequately support this physical activity. When this ability is exceeded, the resultant failure of the spine causes acute and chronic pain, and a reduced capacity to function normally.

It is in everybody's interest, whether employer, employee, or individual, to avoid back injuries by simply 'thinking before lifting'.

Factors associated with back injury

Occupational. Constant manual handling, frequent bending and flexing of the spine, a poor ergonomic workplace, repetitive back movements, all provide a basis for acute injury or chronic complaint.

Personal. Individual strength, age, posture, and degree of fitness are important factors.

Medical/Historical. Previous back complaints, evidence of scoliosis or similar medical conditions, and previous education in back care procedures, will generally, in conjunction with personal factors, dictate the degree of abuse the back can absorb.

The ultimate aim in avoiding back injury is *to identify and eliminate potential risks* before any injury is sustained. To do this effectively, individuals should identify, assess and control any risk factors.

Identify risk factors by reviewing past procedures and comparing the injury rates. Observe and analyse any existing or potential problems. Consider any personal medical or physical limitations. Consult other individuals or organisations.

Assess the risks involved:

- ❏ Is manual handling essential?
- ❏ What options are available?
- ❏ Is the right person involved?

Control any risk by reducing the necessity for manual handling by using alternative means of handling, by maintaining a SAFE work or home environment (no slippery floors or obstructions), and especially by educating all those involved in safe lifting techniques.

When lifting or moving a load, consider not only the weight of the object, but its size and shape, the distance it is to be carried, the height it will have to be lifted, and its position prior to lifting. In fact, does it need lifting or will it be better to push or pull the load?

✔ deposit the load by bending the knees and keeping the back straight (reverse order of lifting)
✔ if pulling or pushing, let the legs do the work

Pregnant women should take special care when lifting, as their spine adjusts to cater for the physical changes of the body. A pregnant woman's ligaments are also affected by hormonal changes and 'soften' considerably. Any heavily pregnant woman who lifts or carries a heavy, restless, wriggling child is at risk of back injury or worse.

Lifting or moving a load
✔ consider the load, – size, shape, etc
✔ consider need for mechanical or manual assistance
✔ position legs apart – one foot level with the load
✔ keep back straight, look up
✔ bend from the hips, avoid 'twisting' the body
✔ tighten the stomach muscles, but don't hold breath
✔ BEND THE KNEES
✔ lift with the legs, not the back
✔ keep the load close to the body
✔ keep carrying distance short
✔ avoid changing grip or 'jerking' the load

INDEX

EMERGENCY NUMBERS

In an emergency go to the nearest telephone and call *'999'* (or **999** or **112** from a mobile phone). Ask for the service that you require (Ambulance – Fire – Police - Coastguard).

Emergency – Ambulance Fire Police 📞 999

NHS Direct 📞 0845 46 47

Doctor _____ 📞 _____ or _____
Address...
....

Dentist _____ 📞 _____ or _____
Address...
....

Hospital – Emergency Number 📞 _____ or _____
Address...
....

Late Night Chemist _____ 📞 _____ or _____
Address...
....

Local Police Station _____ 📞 _____ or _____

Taxi _____ 📞 _____ or _____

Electrical Emergency Service 📞 _____ or _____

Gas Emergency Service 📞 _____ or _____

Water Emergency Service 📞 _____ or _____